# YouTube
## Second Edition

**Digital Media and Society Series**

Nancy Baym, *Personal Connections in the Digital Age*, 2nd edition

Jean Burgess and Joshua Green, *YouTube*, 2nd edition

Mercedes Bunz and Graham Meikle, *The Internet of Things*

Mark Deuze, *Media Work*

Andrew Dubber, *Radio in the Digital Age*

Quinn DuPont, *Cryptocurrencies and Blockchains*

Charles Ess, *Digital Media Ethics*, 2nd edition

Jordan Frith, *Smartphones as Locative Media*

Alexander Halavais, *Search Engine Society*, 2nd edition

Martin Hand, *Ubiquitous Photography*

Robert Hassan, *The Information Society*

Tim Jordan, *Hacking*

Graeme Kirkpatrick, *Computer Games and the Social Imaginary*

Leah A. Lievrouw, *Alternative and Activist New Media*

Rich Ling and Jonathan Donner, *Mobile Communication*

Donald Matheson and Stuart Allan, *Digital War Reporting*

Dhiraj Murthy, *Twitter*, 2nd edition

Jill Walker Rettberg, *Blogging*, 2nd edition

Patrik Wikström, *The Music Industry*, 2nd edition

Zizi A. Papacharissi, *A Private Sphere: Democracy in a Digital Age*

# YouTube

*Online Video and Participatory Culture*

Second Edition

JEAN BURGESS AND
JOSHUA GREEN

polity

First edition published in 2009 by Polity Press
This second edition first published in 2018 by Polity Press

Polity Press
65 Bridge Street
Cambridge CB2 1UR, UK

Polity Press
101 Station Landing
Suite 300
Medford, MA 02155, USA

ISBN-13: 978-0-7456-6018-9 (hardback)
ISBN-13: 978-0-7456-6019-6 (paperback)

A catalogue record for this book is available from the British Library.

Library of Congress Cataloging-in-Publication Data

Names: Burgess, Jean (Jean Elizabeth), author. | Green, Joshua (Joshua Benjamin), author.
Title: Youtube : online video and participatory culture / Jean Burgess, Joshua Green.
Description: Second edition. | Cambridge, UK ; Medford, MA : Polity Press, 2018. | Series: Digital media and society | Includes bibliographical references and index.
Identifiers: LCCN 2018001623 (print) | LCCN 2018003898 (ebook) | ISBN 9781509533596 (Epub) | ISBN 9780745660189 (hardback) | ISBN 9780745660196 (pbk.)
Subjects: LCSH: YouTube (Electronic resource) | Online social networks--Social aspects. | Internet--Social aspects. | Information society.
Classification: LCC HM851 (ebook) | LCC HM851 .B87 2018 (print) | DDC 302.23/1--dc23
LC record available at https://lccn.loc.gov/2018001623

Typeset in 10.25 on 13 pt Scala by
Servis Filmsetting Ltd, Stockport, Cheshire
Printed and bound in Great Britain by Clays Ltd, St. Ives PLC

For further information on Polity, visit our website: politybooks.com

# Contents

# Preface to the Second Edition

The original aim of this book was, as we wrote in the Preface to the first edition, 'to work through some of the often competing ideas about just what YouTube is, and what it might or might not turn out to be for'. We completed the study that it was based on more than a decade ago in 2007, with the book manuscript being delivered a few months later in early 2008.

YouTube has transformed significantly in the past ten years. It has of course continued to grow at dizzying rates, but it has also changed in terms of its business model, its interface and features, its cultural role, and the extent to which it regulates content and behaviour. It has evolved from a disruptive 'Web 2.0' start-up to one of the most powerful platforms in a digital media environment that is dominated by them; and those early competing ideas about what it was, and what it was 'for', while far from settled, are now more widely understood. Given the scope of change since we completed the original manuscript, the project of preparing a second edition might at first glance seem quite daunting. But, despite these significant transformations of the platform, we believe that many of our original findings and arguments have stood the test of time quite well.

First, we stand by our original core argument that YouTube's value – what it had turned out to be 'for' so far – was 'co-created by YouTube Inc., now owned by Google, the users who upload content to the website, and the audiences who engage around that content'. The content contributors even back then were already a diverse group – 'from large media producers and rights-owners such as television stations, sports companies, and major advertisers, to small-to-medium enterprises looking for cheap distribution or alternatives to mainstream broadcast systems, cultural institutions, artists, activists, media literate fans, non-professional and amateur media producers'. Each of these participants, we argued, approached YouTube 'with their own purposes and aims and collectively [shaped] YouTube as a dynamic cultural system'. This is why we said then, and continue to say now, that YouTube was *co-created* by diverse and multiple interests.

We also said that YouTube was a site of participatory culture – and, as we emphasize even more strongly in this edition, *participatory culture is YouTube's core business*. The cultural logics of community, openness, and authenticity are embedded in the YouTube platform and brand at all scales of commerciality, from everyday documentation through to those star YouTubers with six-figure incomes, billions of views and millions of subscribers. However, it is also true that the culture of YouTube – its structure of feeling, to borrow from Raymond Williams – has co-evolved with its growth in scale and commercial maturity. It is our task to tell that story of change over time, as well as to interrogate the emergent politics and contradictions of commercially mediated participatory cultures that the story of YouTube represents so clearly.

Our overall aim in preparing this second edition, then, was to achieve a revised and updated account of the platform, without overwriting the historical record – and certainly without writing an entirely new book. For the most part, we have taken a comparative and additive approach – preserving, updating, and supplementing the original material – but we have tried to be explicit and detailed where possible about how and with what impacts the platform has changed over time. Accordingly, throughout the book we explicitly and reflexively refer to factual statements and arguments that we made in the first edition, and discuss how the scale, characteristics, and significance of the phenomena they refer to have changed.

This comparative and additive approach is of particular importance in Chapter 3, 'YouTube's Popular Culture', which leans heavily on the methods and findings of our original (and non-replicable) content analysis of YouTube's most popular videos, which relied on and critically reflected on the platform's metrics for measuring and representing popularity as they were in 2007. Rather than overwriting that work, we have framed the methods and findings historically, and updated some of the examples. We also show how some of contemporary YouTube's most distinctive and embedded cultural forms, practices, and genres – from vlogging to gameplay and unboxing videos – have emerged from the dynamics of its early popular culture. Early YouTube's popular culture was in turn generated out of the interactions among the affordances and business model of the platform, the activities and interests of content creators, the broader vernacular cultures of the Internet, and the consumption and engagement practices of audiences.

Throughout the book, we have revised the original material for style and tone, as well as updating terminology where it has become dated. For example, you will find fewer references to 'new media' and 'Web 2.0' than in the first edition, except where they refer back to the dominant discourses of the mid-2000s; similarly, we talk about YouTube mostly as a platform rather than a 'website', reflecting the migration to mobile apps and television screens that accounts for so much contemporary YouTube use. We adopt the now-pervasive emic concept of a YouTube 'community' rather than talking about YouTube's 'social network'. Where appropriate, we talk about content creators and channels, rather than users and user profiles, reflecting changes in the way the platform works and the way its cultural logics have changed. Chapter 2 is now entitled 'YouTube and the Media', rather than 'YouTube and the Mainstream Media', because it no longer makes sense to situate YouTube as being separate from the 'mainstream media'. First, YouTube is itself now a dominant media platform in much of the world; second, the broader media environment is now so distributed, digital, multi-platform, and diverse that it would be difficult to say what 'the mainstream media' (as opposed to new or digital media) is.

At the back of the first edition of this book we included two additional commissioned essays, one each by Henry Jenkins and John Hartley. They looked outward from our detailed study of YouTube, which was grounded in the contemporary moment of YouTube's early years, to provide more expansive explorations of the challenges and opportunities that the platform represented to some of the central areas of concern in media and cultural studies – past, present, and future. While the new edition does not include these additional materials, we encourage you to revisit them, and we are forever grateful to Henry and John for contributing their distinctive scholarly insights into YouTube's early cultural significance.

*Jean Burgess, Brisbane, December 2017.*

# Acknowledgements

As well as being the outcome of an intensive collaboration between two colleagues, the original version of this book was the result of a complex empirical research project, which was generously supported institutionally, and which would have been impossible without the help of many other people. It was enabled by a partnership between two institutions on opposite sides of the planet – Queensland University of Technology (QUT) in Brisbane, Australia; and Massachusetts Institute of Technology (MIT) in Cambridge, Massachusetts, USA. The original empirical study around which the book was built was supported by the Australian Research Council Centre of Excellence for Creative Industries and Innovation (CCI) and the Creative Industries Faculty at QUT, and the Program in Comparative Media Studies (CMS) at MIT.

Additionally, some of the data we draw on throughout this book were collected as part of a project completed by the Convergence Culture Consortium. The Consortium was a partnership between MIT's CMS and MTV Networks, Yahoo!, Turner Broadcasting, Fidelity Investments, and GSD&M Idea City. We offer our continued thanks to the coders who, in the years before it was normal for media studies scholars to be equipped with automated methods of content analysis, waded through endless spreadsheets of metadata representing many thousands of YouTube videos of uneven quality and question-able taste: Sam Ford, Eleanor Baird, Lauren Silberman, Xiaochang Li, Ana Domb Krauskopf and Eli Koger. We are grateful to them not only for their hard work but also for their intellectual engagement and spirited contributions to the project. We remain grateful to Rik Eberhardt at CMS for his help collecting and managing the data; Jenny Burton for last-minute editorial assistance; and Paul Brand for his research assistance with the mainstream media representations of YouTube as part of a QUT Creative Industries Faculty Vacation Research Experience Scholarship; we are also grateful to Tim Milfull at QUT for his research assistance with updating the literature base for this edition.

At Polity, we are grateful to our commissioning editor John Thompson for originally championing this project, to Andrea Drugan for supporting it as part of the Digital Media and Society series, to Sarah Lambert for her assistance with the production process; and for their assistance with the second edition, we thank Mary Savigar and Ellen MacDonald-Kramer for their expert assistance as well as their support and encouragement.

We remain grateful to colleagues at our home institutions and around the world, who provided feedback, resources, difficult questions, or moral support the first time around: our thanks go to John Banks, Trine Bjørkmann Berry, Sarah Brouillette, Kate Crawford, Stuart Cunningham, Mark Deuze, Sam Ford, Anne Galloway, Melissa Gregg, Gerard Goggin, Jonathan Gray, Greg Hearn, Helen Klaebe, Kylie Jarrett, Robert Kozinets, Patricia Lange, Jason Potts, Alice Robison, Christina Spurgeon, and Graeme Turner.

The second edition benefited from our connections to a number of dynamic and welcoming research environments. We thank staff and graduate students from the QUT Digital Media Research Centre, especially Stuart Cunningham and his USC Annenberg research and writing partner David Craig; as well as Michael Dezuanni, Nicolas Suzor, Patrik Wikström, Ariadna Matamoros-Fernandez, Jarrod Walczer, Smith Mehta, and Guy Healy for the inspiration their own work on YouTube and other digital media platforms has provided. Microsoft Research provided us with the space and time to work together for a period while Jean was a Visiting

Researcher there in 2013; with respect to platform studies, of which this book is an evolving example, we would like especially to thank Nancy Baym and Tarleton Gillespie for their ongoing support, friendship, and dialogue on related topics.

We owe an eternal debt to our PhD supervisors and post-doctoral mentors Henry Jenkins and John Hartley, who not only generously committed some of their best ideas and formidable energy to this book by providing additional chapters, but who also encouraged and materially supported us to pursue the research collaboration, which began way back in 2007, of which this is the outcome. Henry and John, thank you for trusting us to take on this project, and for supporting us to complete it.

Finally, we would like to thank the unexpectedly large number of colleagues and students who have read, used, and cited the original version of this book (including in one of its three translations), or set it as a text for undergraduate and graduate research students – many of whom have contacted us to enquire about the second edition. We thank you for your patience, and we hope what follows has been worth the wait.

CHAPTER ONE

# How YouTube Matters

This chapter introduces YouTube as an important but complex object of study. It shows how the story of the platform is tied to the story of the changing digital media environment, and to much older debates about the role of media and popular culture in society. The first section discusses YouTube's emergence in the mid 2000s, its subsequent ascendancy to a dominant position in the media environment, and some of the competing public narratives about the reasons for its success. The following section, 'The Platform Business', discusses the changing nature of the media business as it has converged with digital technologies and the Internet, and highlights YouTube's role in those changes. We then describe some of the challenges inherent in studying digital media platforms, and the changing state of the art in YouTube research methods. In the final section, we briefly sketch out some of the scholarly debates about the cultural value of YouTube and its role as a site of 'participatory culture', showing that these debates extend much further back in history than YouTube's period of existence, and that they have relevance well beyond YouTube itself. These are important debates about the importance and value of popular culture, the politics of commercial media, and the significance of ordinary people's access to active and creative participation in culture. YouTube has been a continuous focus of these longstanding debates even as it has evolved along with the changing digital media environment – and that, we argue, is how YouTube matters.

## Origins

Founded by former PayPal employees Chad Hurley, Steve Chen, and Jawed Karim, YouTube's website was officially launched with little public fanfare in June 2005. Its original purpose was, on the surface, a technological rather than a cultural one: YouTube was one of a number of services aiming to remove the technical barriers faced by non-expert users who wanted to share video on the web. The website provided a very simple, integrated interface that enabled people to upload, publish, and view streaming videos without much technical knowledge, using standard web browsers and modest Internet speeds. YouTube set no limits on the number of videos users could upload, offered basic social functions like the opportunity to connect with other users as 'friends', and provided links and HTML code that enabled videos to be easily embedded into other websites. These social networking and sharing features capitalised on and were designed to add value to the recent introduction of popularly accessible blogging platforms like Blogger and Wordpress. Many of these blogging technologies already featured the ability to embed images from popular photosharing platforms like Flickr, a leading 'Web 2.0' service that combined content creation, curation, and social networking. In fact, in 2005, technology business website *TechCrunch* named YouTube as the leading contender to be the 'The Flickr of Video' (Arrington, 2005). This vision of YouTube as a 'Web 2.0' service for videosharing is a long way from the mainstream media platform that YouTube had become by 2017, with its complex relationship to broadcast and cable television and the music business, and with homegrown YouTube stars boasting billions of subscribers.

It would be a mistake to believe that the transformation of YouTube from social networking site to major media platform was master-planned by Hurley, Chen, and Karim, but we do have some information about their thinking in those early days. Fortunately for journalists, researchers, and students of YouTube, the copyright-related court case fought between Google and Viacom resulted in the public release of large numbers of emails sent between the YouTube founders in the early years.[1] As this in-house correspondence shows, while the founders always saw YouTube as a commercial enterprise, they were quite agnostic about the content side of the business – the social networking side came first. That is, mirroring the logics of Web 2.0 at the time, the original vision appeared to be that video content shot on mobile phones would be a catalyst to online connections, perhaps even involving dating, which in turn would increase the size of the YouTube userbase and could generate advertising or subscription revenue. On the distant horizon were more speculative, aspirational ideas about charging their users subscription fees for the ability to watch 'premium' media content. Pitching for investment at Sequoia Capital in 2005,[2] the founders hinted that amateur content created and contributed by ordinary, socially networked users might eventually sit alongside legitimately uploaded, professionally produced media content; meanwhile, the emails simultaneously reveal some nervousness about copyright violating user-uploaded content. But overall, within certain limits (particularly with respect to violent and sexually explicit content), in practice YouTube really didn't mind what kind of content their users were uploading, as long as the scale of the platform's user population and their activity levels continued to grow. This relative openness, both in terms of what content was uploaded to the platform, and who got to upload it, was embedded in the company aim, which was included in the presentation slides ('pitch deck') and press release accompanying their (ultimately successful) pitch to Sequoia Capital:

> To become the primary outlet of user-generated content on the Internet, and to allow anyone to upload, share, and browse this content.

In a later slide from the pitch deck, the founders emphasised the platform's key affordances, which combined its fundamental technical features (making it easier for ordinary users to upload, transcode, and share video online) with a community-formation function:

- Consumers upload their videos to YouTube. YouTube takes care of serving the content to millions of viewers.
- YouTube's video encoding back-end converts uploaded videos to Flash Video.
- YouTube provides a community that connects users to videos, users to users, and videos to videos.

This aspect of the pitch aligns early YouTube with the tech industry and 'Web 2.0', because it emphasises usable functionality, technical features, and content as a means of social connection.

But from the beginning, YouTube was actively engaged in a convergence between tech industry and media industries ways of thinking and operating. The Sales and Distribution plan presented in the Sequoia pitch shows that the company sought to combine advertising revenue generated from user activity and/or fees for premium features (a social networking site business model) with subscription or hosting fees for premium content (a media business model):

- Advertising
- Act as a for-pay distribution channel for promotional videos
- Charge members for premium features
- Charge viewers for premium content

Here too, albeit in an early form, we can see the uneasy convergence between the dual logics of community and commerce; and broadcast and social media – logics that still persisted, competed, and conflicted in the YouTube of 2017.

YouTube has come a long way since 2005. In October 2006, Google acquired the business for $1.65 billion.[3] By November 2007 it was already the most popular entertainment website in Britain, with the BBC website in second place,[4] and in early 2008 it was, according to various web metrics services, consistently in the top ten most-visited websites globally. In 2017 it was ranked second behind only Google worldwide, with more than 85 per cent of visitors coming from outside the United States.[5] When we completed the first edition of this manuscript in April 2008, YouTube hosted upwards of 85 million videos, a number that represented a tenfold increase over the previous year (and one that seemed jaw-droppingly huge at the time).[6] The growth in both content and user-base has continued at such a rate that the company has had to find new ways to measure and communicate its scale – merely counting videos soon became inadequate to convey the platform's growing market power. By 2013, YouTube was reporting that more than 100 hours of video were uploaded each minute;[7] and in 2017 the company website claimed that their billion users were watching a billion hours of content each day.[8] In 2008, Internet market research company com-Score reported that the service accounted for 37 per cent of all Internet videos watched inside the United States, with the next largest service, Fox Interactive Media, accounting for only 4.2 per cent.[9] By 2017, even given the proliferation of competing video apps and streaming services like Netflix, YouTube reportedly accounted for 80 per cent of the total 12 billion hours spent using the top 10 video streaming apps on the Android mobile platform in the twelve months to July 2017 (Perez, 2017). According to a music industry report, YouTube even accounted for 46 per cent of all online music streaming time in 2017, including non-video platforms like Pandora and Spotify (McIntyre, 2017). As a media platform whose early, dramatic growth was substantially driven by user-created and user-curated content, YouTube's sheer size and mainstream popularity remain unprecedented.

Since the original features of the YouTube platform were very similar to other online video start-ups, various commentators have sought to explain how it so rapidly overtook the competition in that first year. As told by Jawed Karim, the third co-founder who left the business to return to college in

November 2005, the success of the site is due to the implementation of four key features: video recommendations via the 'related videos' list; an email link to enable video sharing; comments (and other social networking functionality); and an embeddable video player (Gannes, 2006). These features were implemented as part of a redesign after the failure of previous attempts to popularise the website; attempts that included offering $100 to attractive girls who posted ten or more videos. According to Karim, the founders reportedly didn't receive a single reply to this offer, which they posted on Craigslist (Gannes, 2006).[10]

An alternative story about the tipping point in YouTube's journey to early success is a cultural rather than a technological one. It relates to a satirical sketch from *Saturday Night Live* featuring two nerdy, stereotypical New Yorkers rapping about buying cupcakes and going to see the *Chronicles of Narnia*. In December 2005 this clip – entitled 'Lazy Sunday' – became something of a break-out YouTube hit. The two-and-a-half-minute sketch was viewed 1.2 million times in its first ten days online and had been seen more than five million times by February 2006, when NBC Universal demanded YouTube remove it, along with 500 other clips, or face legal action under the Digital Millennium Copyright Act (Biggs, 2006). The rise and fall of 'Lazy Sunday' brought YouTube to the notice of the mainstream press – and as something other than a technological development. For the *New York Times* (Biggs, 2006), 'Lazy Sunday' demonstrated the potential of YouTube as an outlet for established media to reach out to the elusive but much-desired youth audience. As much as it was imagined to be a viral marketing wonderland, however, the site was reported as a looming threat to the established logics of the broadcast media landscape (Kerwin, 2006; Wallenstein, 2006a). Although early reporting in the features, technology, and business pages discussed YouTube and video sharing as the Internet's next 'new thing' (Byrne, 2005; Graham, 2005; Kirsner, 2005; Nussenbaum, Ryan, and Lewis, 2005;

Rowan, 2005), it was through this 'big media'-related event that YouTube became a regular *subject* for the mainstream media.

Quite apart from which one of these origin myths turned out to be right, it is significant that each of them evokes a different idea of what early YouTube was: was it another online fad, beloved by the tech crowd, that ordinary people needed to be convinced to use? Or a new kind of media distribution and talent discovery platform, sort of like television, but on the web? Either way, YouTube's early ascendancy occurred amid a fog of public uncertainty and contradiction around what it was actually *for*. In August 2005, only a few months into the life of the service, the 'About Us' page offered only the most tentative and vague hints at the possible uses of YouTube:

> Show off your favorite videos to the world
> Take videos of your dogs, cats, and other pets
> Blog the videos you take with your digital camera or cell phone
> Securely and privately show videos to your friends and family around the world
> . . . and much, much more!

In these early days, the website carried the by-line 'Your Digital Video Repository', which conflicts somewhat with the now-notorious exhortation to 'Broadcast Yourself' – a catch-phrase that has passed into vernacular use, but which hasn't been a prominent part of YouTube's brand identity since it was dropped from the logo in 2010. This shift from the idea of the website as a personal storage facility for video content to a platform for public self-expression opened it up to the more revolutionary rhetoric about user-led content creation and innovation that led to *Time* making the person of the year 'You' in 2006 (Grossman, 2006b). Since then, YouTube's apparent or stated mission has continuously evolved as a result of the similarly changing relationships and tensions among competing corporate logics, changing platform affordances, and diverse user practices.

Despite this hype around a user-generated content revolution, and the company's insistence that the service was designed for sharing personal videos among existing social networks, it was to be a combination of the mass popularity of particular user-created videos and the ability to watch mainstream media content that made YouTube a dominant platform, serving the interests of the company by building audience scale. It is also this combination of self-expression and commercial media culture that has positioned YouTube as a key site of conflicts over copyright, the politics of participatory culture, and the governance structures of digital media platforms, all of which are discussed in further detail in the following chapters.

## The Platform Business

From launch, YouTube presented itself as a neutral web service for sharing and viewing content, rather than as a content producer itself. In a 2005 press release announcing the $3.5m investment from Sequoia Capital, the focus was squarely on scale (of both the content and the social network), saying that they were 'moving eight terabytes of data per day through the YouTube community – the equivalent of moving one Blockbuster store a day over the Internet'.[11] YouTube was a real-world example of David Weinberger's (2007) model of the 'meta businesses' – the '[then]-new category of business that enhances the value of information developed elsewhere and thus benefits the original creators of that information' (224). Weinberger's examples included Apple's iTunes store, which profited through music purchases but didn't bear the costs of discovery and production the way that record labels did; rather, iTunes made aggregated information about music 'more searchable, more findable, and more usable' (225).

So too, YouTube performed a content discovery role, attracting the attention of audiences, and in turn offering some content contributors revenue streams from advertising sold on the website. At the same time the platform actively invited and encouraged a wide range of participants to upload their own content and form social connections. It is an early, paradigmatic example of the transition from two-sided to multi-sided media markets (Wikström, 2013). In two-sided markets, like the traditional media business model for news-papers, the media outlet needs to balance the interests of advertisers on one 'side', and readers or audiences on the other. Multi-sided markets (such as for complex software packages or social media platforms) are built around a mix of participants with diverse interests, contributing to and extracting value from the core product or service at different points (Wikström, 2013: 236). In the contemporary digital media environment, most of the focus in business innovation has been on the development of platforms that attempt to coordinate, serve, and attempt to profit from these complex, multi-sided interactions among stakeholders. In YouTube's case, these include: audiences; amateur, pro-amateur, and professional content creators; media partners; advertisers; new intermediaries like the multi-channel networks (MCNs); and third-party developers.

As Burgess (2015) has discussed elsewhere, as part of the shift to multi-sided markets, the mid to late 2000s through to the mid 2010s saw the rise of a *platform paradigm* – 'a way of organising our *thinking* about the social media landscape as much as it is a way of organising the burgeoning *business* of connecting users with their creative content and each other'. Along the same lines, Anne Helmond describes this shift as the 'platformisation' of the Internet – 'the rise of the platform as the dominant infrastructural and economic model of the social web' (Helmond, 2015). Under the platform paradigm, much of our social and cultural activity is mediated by devices and soft-ware applications (platforms) owned by a small number of very large companies – including, in the West, Google/Alphabet (who owns YouTube) and Facebook; and in China, TenCent (who owns WeChat, QQ). Most of the platforms provided by these companies were originally built around a simple set of communicative functions and the progressive convergence of content creation, consumption, interpersonal and public communication (Burgess, 2017). Some of them (particularly Facebook and WeChat) have significantly expanded their operations so that, while media content, advertising, and social connection remain core, their business interests and activities now connect high-end data science, location-based retail tracking, personal finance, infrastructure, and logistics – on a 'planetary scale' (Rossiter, 2016).

In an influential early article and more recent work, Tarleton Gillespie (2010; 2017) has critiqued the way that the platform companies deploy the many available metaphorical meanings of the term 'platform' to serve a wide variety of interests and appease different stakeholders at once. Platforms also rely on the idea that they are neutral intermediaries to devolve responsibility for content and behaviour to their users and partners. But as Philip Napoli and Robyn Caplan have argued (2017), the self-positioning of digital media platforms as tech companies rather than as media companies was always somewhat disingenuous, and it is no longer sustainable. While YouTube for many years managed to maintain an image of itself as a neutral platform for sharing content, rather than a content provider, there can no longer be any denying that it does both – a fact that has important ramifications for the extent to which it is subject to media policy and content regulation. At the same time, platforms shape and govern the media environment, actively regulating their users' content and behaviour through increasingly complex sociotechnical mechanisms of control (Gillespie, 2017).

In the twelve years since it was first launched to 2017, YouTube has become increasingly engaged in the media business. Accordingly, the platform has become less chaotic and more 'formalised' (Burgess, 2012a). It has matured as a company and has increasingly introduced structured business arrangements and practices aimed at professionalising, ordering, and regulating the content that is published to the platform. In doing so, it has become more focused on exploiting a range of emerging advertising and subscription-based revenue streams. Some of the greatest changes to the service have been motivated by a desire to make the platform more appealing to potential advertisers and media partners – from the introduction of the Content ID system for copyright enforcement, to the extensive display and interactive advertising products, guidelines for crafting effective brand channels, and premium channel options allowing content creators or publishers to wrap their channels in branding. The company has become increasingly proactive in supporting creative production and developing original content. A noteworthy development in 2011 was YouTube's $100 million investment in original content support (Vascellaro, Efrati, and Smith, 2011) – the beginning of their strong push in this direction. The program includes support and promotion for content creators with good prospects for scaling up their audiences, the creation of YouTube-owned studio spaces and artist development programs available to these up-and-coming YouTubers, as well as outreach to Hollywood casting agencies, production companies, and stars; and more recent moves into original programming and enhanced fan engagement features on the subscription-based YouTube Red sub-platform have been squarely focused around previously amateur and now professional media stars who have built their careers on the YouTube platform (Popper, 2015). Through this process of experimentation with formalising and commercialising the platform, YouTube has helped redefine what 'professional media' looks like – and sometimes, it looks like videoblogging, live gameplay, haul videos, beauty tips, and toy unboxing videos. These home-grown YouTube genres, enacted by star YouTubers and cross-platform influencers, form part of the new industry sector that YouTube and its user community have helped co-create, and that Stuart Cunningham and David Craig (2017) call 'social media entertainment'.

There have always been two simultaneously operating YouTubes: one oriented towards professional production, with the requisite issues of copyright protection, professional aesthetics, and the challenges of commercialising reach and attention; and one more interested in sheer scale and near-ubiquity, providing a platform for everyday expression, vernacular creativity, and community formation. The two YouTubes have never really been separate, and are increasingly entangled. Indeed, it is the dynamic tensions and synergies between them that have animated YouTube's growth, diversity, and change over time as a platform; and both have always had a commercial side. In mapping out the terrain of social media entertainment, Stuart Cunningham et al. (2016) point to the dynamic tension between, on the one hand, the 'NoCal' or Northern Californian business model and ideology associated with the tech industry and Silicon Valley; and the 'SoCal' or Southern Californian business model and ideology associated with the major media players and Hollywood. The tensions between these competing logics have always defined and animated the culture and business of the platform.

Because of these competing logics, YouTube's economic, cultural, and social value has never been produced solely or even predominantly by its corporate strategy and business practices. Rather, YouTube's diverse culture and value have been collectively co-created by its users (including audiences, content creators, and intermediaries), via their consumption, evaluation, and entrepreneurial activities, within the shifting architectures and affordances of the platform. The platform's distinctive brand value fundamentally relies on its co-creative dynamics and its vernacular cultures. For YouTube, then, *participatory culture is core business*. But the question is, who gets to participate in the business? Under what conditions, with what impacts on culture and society, and in whose interests do they participate? And how have these dynamics changed over time? In addressing these societally significant questions empirically, we need to draw on a range of disciplines and methods.

## Studying YouTube

The original edition of this book was the first attempt to treat YouTube in itself as an object of study. At the time, there was not yet much of a sense of a shared understanding of YouTube's cultural uses and dynamics (or even of what exactly it *was*), and we wanted to change that. There were few other serious analyses of YouTube's cultural meanings and uses available when we began this project in 2007. Since 2009, there has been this book, as well as a few others (see Lange, 2014; Snickars and Vonderau, 2009; and Strangelove, 2010). But at the time, writing a whole book about a single platform (rather than, say, a medium or sub-sector of a media industry, like television) was at best a novel thing to do; at worst, it looked like a mistake that risked capture by a particular corporate brand, resulting in a failure to attend to the historical and political forces behind it. Nevertheless, we felt that attempting to systematically study YouTube as a platform was both a useful way to understand the historical development of digital media, and a significant and worthy scholarly challenge in itself.

Writing about the methodological challenges of making sense of television nearly three decades ago, Stephen Heath described it as:

> a somewhat difficult object, unstable, all over the place, tending derisively to escape anything we say about it: given the speed of its changes (in technology, economics, programming), its interminable flow (of images and sounds, their endlessly disappearing present), its quantitative everydayness (the very quality of this medium each and every day). (Heath, 1990: 267)

YouTube was in 2007 and remains in 2017 an even more unstable object of study, marked by dynamic change (both in terms of videos and organisation), a similar quotidian frequency, or 'everydayness' to television, and an almost incomprehensibly large and highly diverse archive of video content. From the beginning, it was further complicated by its dual function as both a 'top-down' platform for the distribution of popular culture and a 'bottom-up' platform for vernacular creativity; and the ongoing blurring of the boundaries between the two. It was variously understood as a distribution platform that could make the products of commercial media more easily accessible, challenging the promotional reach the mass media had been accustomed to monopolising, while at the same time it was being celebrated as a platform for user-created content where challenges to existing forms of commercial media might emerge, be they independent modes of producing traditional media genres like news or music videos, or new genres like vlogging or 'live' gameplay.

Secondly, given the rise of the 'platform paradigm' discussed in the previous section, it is important to understand what these platforms are, and how they work. The digital or social media platforms provided by these companies share certain 'social media logics' (van Dijck and Poell, 2013), like connectivity, datafication, and convergence. But each specific platform also mediates, coordinates, and controls content and interactions in a specific way; and each has its own distinctive culture of use. In fact, it no longer makes much sense to talk about 'the web' or 'the Internet', or 'video' without reference to specific platforms. It is important to understand the distinctive affordances of each platform, their cultures of use and social norms, and how the co-evolution of their business models, technologies, and uses are shaping and reshaping media and communication.

Our ambition to contribute to a more comprehensive understanding of YouTube as a platform required dealing with both specificity and scale, because YouTube's culture was very diverse and its population of users and content library were enormous. The original research project therefore presented us with some methodological challenges. The methods of cultural and media studies (like textual analysis and ethnography) are useful for specificity – they enable the close, richly contextualised analysis of the local and the particular, bringing this close analysis into dialogue with context. At the qualitative end of the methodological spectrum, Patricia Lange's (2007a; 2007b; 2014) ethnographic work with the 'first generation video bloggers' who did so much to construct and reflect on the idea of a YouTube community has produced a number of important insights into the ways YouTube operates as a social networking site for certain participants, and the rich mundanity of the communicative practices that take place there. Most importantly, her work insistently reminds us of the need to consider fully the lived experience and materiality of everyday cultural practice. Lange's work has been particularly important to this book because it gave us supplementary tools with which to think about the *uses* of YouTube by real people as part of everyday life.

But scale even at the relatively modest level of 'early YouTube' tested the limits of these grounded, textured accounts of specific texts, genres, or practices. If we had decided at the outset that we were interested in exploring remix culture, or music fandom, or foot fetish videos, or DIY cooking shows, or any number of other niche uses of YouTube, we would have been sure to find sufficient examples for a journal article among the millions of videos available on the platform at the time we undertook the study. But the challenge we set ourselves in this book required us to get beyond the level of particular examples or themes associated with pre-existing debates in media studies, so that approach would not have been helpful. We therefore needed to find a way to engage with a broad sweep of YouTube's content, treating the content as digital traces of its cultures of use, without predetermining what those uses were – taking us beyond small-scale, manual methods, and into the realm of computer-assisted or digital methods.

When we started this project, approaches to YouTube that used computational methods to study it as a 'whole system' were restricted to the 'harder' or more positivist end of social science – usually, from computer science and informatics, employing methodological tools like social network analysis (Cha et al., 2007; Gill et al., 2007). These studies revealed content patterns, explored the popularity life-cycles of videos across the website, and mapped the *behavioural* patterns of users based on the traces that they leave behind. This kind of work was to become more prominent and used across a wide range of disciplines with the emergence of Twitter as a large-scale platform for public communication towards the end of the 2000s, and it is now ubiquitous in Internet studies and communication research.

Digital methods draw heavily on the most obvious and accessible features of the information architecture of the platform under study. For example, in YouTube, early studies used hyperlink analysis to map large-scale patterns in connections between videos or users (Cha et al., 2007), but only where those connections had already been 'hard-wired' as hyperlinks. Early in the platform's life, much of this large-scale, computer-assisted research relied on YouTube's native categorisation and tagging systems, which enable uploaders to freely describe and sort their videos by content, theme, and style. The limited choices of categories YouTube provided, with titles such as 'Pets & Animals' and 'Cars & Vehicles', at best offered a very general framework for organising content across the website; and one that was imposed by design rather than emerging organically out of collective practice. In 2017, YouTube's categories remain broad, and formal changes to the organisational hierarchy of the site have significantly downplayed these categories as a key way for users to discover videos. Whereas they were previously presented on the front page to users as a potential starting point, these categories have been progressively obscured – to begin with, as part of the drive to move users towards search and personalised recommendations. Later, YouTube's interface began to group featured content into simplified, company-curated 'channels', which appropriated the names of most of the original, user-assigned categories. This means that platform-provided metadata and categories are both subject to change and highly influential over what kinds of digital methods research can be done.

Similarly, the strategic use of the website's tagging functionality – where uploaders apply popular but perhaps inaccurate tags and titles to content and mark videos as responses to popular but unrelated content in order to increase the chances of a video being seen – make empirical analyses of YouTube based primarily on those data problematic, especially if the data points or categories are taken at face value, without an understanding of the platform's cultures of use. The newer sub-field of critical digital methods is beginning to make use of YouTube's in-built metrics, algorithms, and ontologies, accessed via the API, and combining this data analysis with critical software studies (Rieder et al., 2017; Burgess and Matamoros-Fernandéz, 2016). These kinds of critical digital methods are sometimes performed under the rubric of 'platform studies' (Plantin et al., 2016), or 'interface methods' (Marres and Gerlitz, 2016) – that is, methods that draw on the data generated by platforms while also treating the platforms themselves critically (see also Rieder et al., 2017). However, effectively combining digital methods with close, qualitative approaches to social interactions and critical analysis of digital media content remains an ongoing challenge. Attempting to address the missing middle between large-scale quantitative analysis and the sensitivity of qualitative methods, our original empirical study began with a content analysis of 4,320 of the videos calculated to be 'most popular' on the website for a discrete period – between August and November 2007. We used an automated web scraper to gather the metadata and links to each video, but we analysed them manually. This approach provided a way to order a relatively large body of raw material without selecting it in advance, so that we were able to identify patterns across the sample, as well as to interrogate clusters of individual texts using our much more familiar qualitative methods. While the bulk of the findings is discussed in Chapter 3, we drew on examples from the dataset throughout the book, for purposes such as identifying controversies and mapping aesthetic characteristics across particular cultural forms. The original study enabled us to identify, for the first time, some key patterns in the composition of YouTube's 'common culture' across a number of elements (amateur vs traditional media content; and the most significant forms, genres, and practices). We were also able to reflect critically on the role of sociotechnical features of the platform, including its metrics and the user interface, in shaping popularity. As a supplementary exercise, we studied the public representations and understandings of YouTube via the thematic analysis of a corpus of mainstream press articles about YouTube that were published between 2006–7. The results and a number of key examples from this sub-project are discussed in Chapter 2.

The study, driven especially by the content analysis, sought not only to map and measure the extent of popularity of particular forms and uses of early YouTube, but also to use the findings to better understand the emerging issues for the cultural politics of digital media. Moving back and forth between the empirical findings of this study, critical discussion of the current public debates, and the insights provided by other YouTube scholars whose work is grounded in media and cultural studies perspectives, this book places YouTube into dialogue with the central problems of media and cultural studies around the politics of popular culture, citizenship, and media power. These are the questions that are invoked by the concept of 'participatory culture'.

## The Politics of Participatory Culture

The term 'participatory culture' was used prevalently in the 2000s to talk about the apparent link between more accessible digital technologies, user-created content, and shifts in the power relations between media industries and their consumers (see especially Jenkins, 2006a), in relation to the emergence of what we now call social media platforms. Jenkins' definition of a 'participatory culture' is one in which 'fans and other consumers are invited to actively participate in the creation and circulation of new content' (Jenkins, 2006a: 290). This might seem at first like a rather comfortable arrangement (and one which Jenkins presents as a potential rather than present reality), but YouTube proves that in practice the economic and cultural rearrangements that 'participatory culture' stands for are as disruptive and uncomfortable as they might be potentially liberating. The popular media debates and struggles around YouTube that we discuss in the following chapters are less about technology and more about the normative cultural and political questions that the original formulations of participatory culture lay out (see Jenkins et al., 2006): who gets to speak, and who gets the attention; what compensations or rewards there are for creativity and work; and the uncertainties around various forms of expertise and authority. These are all questions that have come up repeatedly in debates about the value and legitimacy of popular culture.

The politics of popular culture have had a long and contested history in the academic field of Cultural Studies (Storey, 2003). For cultural studies theorists at various times, culture was both 'ordinary' (Hoggart, 1957; Williams, 1958) and a potential site of symbolic struggle, empowerment, or self-expression (Fiske, 1989; 1992a). For these theorists, popular culture mattered as part of a political project, but not usually for its own sake. This was a point made with searing clarity in Stuart Hall's famous (1981) statement that:

> Popular culture is one of the sites where this struggle for and against a culture of the powerful is engaged: it is also the stake to be won or lost in that struggle. It is the arena of

> consent and resistance. It is partly where hegemony arises, and where it is secured. It is not a sphere where socialism, a socialist culture – already fully formed – might be simply 'expressed'. But it is one of the places where socialism might be constituted. That is why 'popular culture' matters. Otherwise, to tell you the truth, I don't give a damn about it. (Hall, 1981: 239)

These long-standing struggles over the politics of the popular in modernity have left a legacy in the competing definitions of popular culture operating in the twenty-first century. On the one hand, popular culture has most commonly been thought of – often pejoratively – in terms of mass commercial, consumer culture – reality TV, shopping malls, celebrity gossip, the Top 40, and videogames – and in the twenty-first century, much of the commercial social media ecology would fit this category as well. Under this definition, popular culture is distinct from traditional high culture through its conditions of production and consumption within capitalism, as well as its aesthetics and associated identities. A second way of understanding popular culture is as 'the culture of the people' – authentic, organic, everyday culture, distinct from *both* high culture and commercial popular culture. Both of these definitions of the popular, and the politics that go along with them, cropped up in the public discourses around YouTube in its early years.

In the context of digital media, liberal and progressive ideologies about popular culture have also become inextricably linked with Silicon Valley capitalism, and are therefore part of YouTube's DNA as a platform. As Fred Turner has argued (2006), the Silicon Valley ideology that produced most of the early twenty-first century's dominant social media platforms relies on the West Coast counterculture's residual desire for folk culture, later articulated to technoculture and US individualism to produce a specific kind of 'digital utopianism' (F. Turner, 2006) that was the precursor to the contemporary techno-libertarianism that characterises many of these companies today. It also underpins some of the more celebratory and optimistic accounts around the democratisation of cultural production that – back in the mid 2000s – many commentators hoped Web 2.0 was to bring (e.g. Benkler, 2006: 274–8; and Jenkins, 2006a: 135–7).

However, as Burgess has discussed elsewhere (2006), the exponential growth of more mundane and formerly private forms of 'vernacular creativity' as part of public culture, as evident in the growth of online social networks, blogs, photo-sharing, and videoblogging (Berry, 2015); the incorporation of user-generated content in the logics of public service broad-casting throughout the 2000s; the new business models associated with Web 2.0 that focused on infrastructure for user-generated content and social networking (O'Reilly, 2005); and the attempts of brand capitalism to manufacture bottom-up engagement through viral marketing (Spurgeon, 2008) – all these demonstrated that there was a broader 'participatory turn' taking place, so that the two opposing definitions of the popular were converging – even if their *poli-tics* were still up for grabs. Everyday creativity began to occupy central stage in discussions of the media industries and their future in the context of digital culture. Consumption was no longer necessarily seen as the end point in an economic chain of production but as a dynamic site of innovation and growth in itself (Bruns, 2008; Potts et al., 2008b), and this extended to the practices of media consumers or audiences (see Hartley, 2004; Green and Jenkins, 2009). Further, the practices of fan communities were becoming increas-ingly incorporated within the logics of the media industries (Green and Jenkins, 2009; Jenkins, 2006b: 144–9; Murray, 2004; Shefrin, 2004). Increasingly, more sophisticated narratives, which rewarded the close attention and repeated viewing associated with media fandom, were becoming more commonplace (Mittell, 2006; Jenkins 2006a), and the committed, attentive, and often productive practices of fans provided models for desired audience and consumer behaviour in a wider range of industries (Gray, Sandvoss, and Harrington, 2008).

In *The Wealth of Networks*, Yochai Benkler's (2006) enthusiasm about the possibilities of the new networks of social production relied on an imagined opposition between a pre-industrial folk culture and the alienation of twentieth-century mass popular culture, which, he argued, 'displaced' folk culture and transformed individuals and communities from 'coproducers and replicators to passive consumers' (Benkler, 2006: 296). This claim that the emergence of peer-produced culture represented a renaissance of folk culture reproduces too simplistic a divide between the two definitions of popular culture – the culture of the people on the one hand, and commercial or industrial popular culture on the other. The story of YouTube is the story of the convergences between the two, and the frictions and tensions that result.

Early YouTube illustrated the increasingly complex relations among producers and consumers in the creation of meaning, value, and agency engendered by the relative flatness of social media platforms. Along its twelve-year lifespan, we can see new and shifting convergences among personal, private, and public life; and between commercial and amateur content creation and audience engagement. In public and scholarly debates, the role of platforms in aggregating and exploiting data, and using algorithmic means to curate and shape our experience in ways that also serve their business logics (or the interests of their parent companies), have also come much more to the fore.

YouTube is experienced in a range of different ways by different users – it has always been a platform for amateur and professional production and distribution, creative consumption, fandom, curation, and critique – and ordinary audience enjoyment. YouTube has increased the scale and complexity of both its commercial practices and the controls it exerts over the conditions of participation in the platform, but it has an absolute commercial imperative to be seen to support its core cultural logics of community, authenticity, and vernacular culture. These tensions have been the source of YouTube's cultural generativity and growth, as well as the cause of many of the struggles among stakeholders and regulatory regimes that characterise its politics as a platform. These tensions around the politics of commercial participatory culture highlight the diverse and highly significant ways YouTube matters – to culture, society, and the economy.

# CHAPTER TWO

# YouTube and the Media

This chapter is focused on YouTube's evolving relationship with the surrounding media environment – a relationship that has several distinctive but interlocking aspects. We begin the chapter with a discussion of how early YouTube was framed by the 'traditional' or 'mainstream' media, who reported on and constructed meanings for what was then a new and exotic cultural phenomenon. The next section of the chapter focuses specifically on the discourses of youth and 'media panic' that were significant in this early reporting. Later sections focus on how talent and cultural practices flowed back and forth between YouTube's vernacular culture and traditional broadcast media systems; then, how copyright has been a site of struggle between YouTube and traditional media industries as well as between YouTube and YouTubers. Finally, we discuss how YouTube became increasingly entangled and co-dependent on the formalised media industries before becoming a powerful, mainstream media platform in its own right – along the way participating in the transformation of the media business itself.

## Framing YouTube

By 2007, YouTube had already disrupted existing media business models and had emerged as a new site of media power. It had received significant press attention, and was now a mainstream player in the digital media industry, but it was also regularly used as a vehicle for rehearsing public debates about new media and the Internet as a disruptive force on business and society, particularly with regard to young people. In this section, we revisit some of the ideas that underpinned these early media representations of the platform, and consider YouTube's evolving position in the changing digital media environment.

In engaging with these debates, we draw on our thematic analysis (completed in 2007) of how the press and television news media covered YouTube in its first two years of existence. What emerged is a set of issues that lined up with traditional news values, and that worked to shore up the interests of the incumbent media. The then-novel platform tended to be framed either as a chaotic and unregulated repository for a flood of amateur content, or (in Business sections particularly) as a big new player in the digital economy. These definitional frames resulted in a steady but repetitive stream of news stories clustering around some familiar themes: youth, celebrity, and morality on the one hand; copyright law and the media or technology business on the other.

These debates, however familiar, contributed to forming and bedding down the public's understanding of what YouTube was and what mattered about it. Media framing and reality create each other, forming a dynamic feedback loop, so that the mainstream or incumbent media's early struggles to comprehend and make sense of the meanings and implications of YouTube not only reflected public concerns, but also helped to produce them. The repetitive framing of YouTube as an amateur 'free-for-all', for instance, shaped the agenda around concerns with lawlessness, the crisis of expertise, and the collapse of cultural value. As YouTube has built an increasingly sophisticated advertising platform and courted professional producers and large entertainment companies, the company has worked somewhat concertedly to shift this framing in all its public messaging, while retaining the vernacular flavour that has made it distinctive.

Similarly, mainstream media discourses about YouTube helped to frame the problems that later became matters of material concern for policy and law, and consequently shaped the changing affordances and protocols of the platform itself. So, for example, concerns about copyright 'piracy', antisocial behaviour or exploitation of vulnerable young people mean that regulatory interventions are required – like blocking YouTube on school computers to protect children and young people from cyberbullying, premature sexualisation, or exposure to commercialism.

One of the most striking things about early mainstream reporting of YouTube is the degree to which these news frames conflicted with one another. For example, on New Year's Eve 2007, Australian current affairs programs *Today Tonight* and *A Current Affair* both broadcast stories about the most popular YouTube clips of the preceding year, describing the website as both a repository for 'amazing, embarrassing, and sometimes downright dangerous moments' around the world, and a launching platform for 'many new stars' ('YouTube's Most Watched', 2007; 'Best YouTube Videos', 2007). At such times YouTube was framed positively, and was represented as a site of wacky, weird, and wonderful user-generated content, some of which might go viral, and lead to the discovery of talented new stars. Within only a few weeks, however, the same programs returned to business-as-usual stories about YouTube, framing it as a very bad object indeed – an under-regulated site of lawless, unethical, and even pathological behaviour centred around youth, categorised as both a vulnerable group and a source of trouble.

As YouTube has evolved, so too has its role in the cycles of news reporting: from being described as one among a plethora of novel 'Web 2.0' applications and a potential site of ordinary self-expression, to its prominence as a threat to media dominance and civil order, and, more recently, as a major media company in its own right. By 2017, broadcast media were continuing to celebrate YouTube with regular birthday specials and retrospectives – often run as 'human interest' stories in television news and current affairs programs, which also help to memorialise it, and to reinforce a narrative of progress from primitive and amateur to slick and professional, from trivial and niche to mass popular.

## Social Anxieties and Media Panics

In the popular imagination, YouTube has always been connected to persistent social anxieties, particularly about young people and digital media. The narrative tropes that go along with these anxieties are characterised by the particularly modern convergence of 'trouble-as-fun, fun-as-trouble' that Hebdige (1988: 30) saw in media images of youth in postwar Britain – where young people were represented as an exotic other, at once exuberantly creative and dangerous. Images of youth have long been closely associated with ideas about shifts in capitalism and the organisation of social structures such as class, wealth distribution, and consumption practices (Murdock and McCron, 1976: 10), and where new media are seen as key disruptive agents, the two are often conflated. Indeed, Kirsten Drotner (2000: 150) argues that young people are connected to media by complementary metaphors of newness and change, and because of this, discourses around youth and discourses around new media inevitably become entangled. In the case of YouTube the 'trouble-as-fun, fun-as-trouble' convergence is further amplified through adult anxieties about an 'intergenerational [digital] divide' mobilised through discourses of 'technological exoticism' (Herring, 2008), where *both* YouTube and the masses of 'youth' assumed to be its default users, are undisciplined, savage, and at the same time new and exciting (Driscoll and Gregg, 2008). This is apparent even in seemingly positive arguments about young people's 'natural' technological prowess, such as Prensky's (2001a; 2001b) frustratingly persistent notion of the 'digital native', which still underpins so much talk of media 'generations' (Burgess, 2016).

While much of this anxiety centred around adolescents

early on, in recent years, heightened concerns around risk and safety for younger children have emerged as YouTube has become more mundane and embedded in everyday life, and as it has become available on mobile screens. YouTube is formally restricted to people thirteen years and older, but is hugely popular with kids far younger than that, whether watching with their parents and peers or on their own. One solution to this has been the YouTube Kids app, a mobile-only, advertising-supported version of the YouTube platform for children three to five years old that was launched in February 2015,[1] with embedded parental controls (such as a timer, and ability to toggle search on or off), populated with pre-curated content (Shribman 2015; Kleeman, 2015). But whether inside or outside the walled garden, the huge popularity of toy unboxing videos with young kids and the rise of social media influencer channels aimed at or featuring young children raise regulatory concerns in markets that have controls aimed at restricting advertising to children (Campbell, 2016; Craig and Cunningham, 2017). There are also persistent adult anxieties about children inadvertently being exposed to inappropriate content, not only through the platform's regular recommended videos or search algorithms, but even through the YouTube Kids app (see, for example, Laura June's (2017) exposé of the 'Fake Peppa Pig problem').

Many of the earliest news stories about YouTube followed the pattern of the 'moral panic' – a term which has now passed into everyday language but which in cultural studies is used to describe a specific cycle of co-influence between media representation and social reality around issues of public concern (Cohen, 1972). In the landmark cultural studies text *Policing the Crisis*, Stuart Hall et al. (1978) analysed the way mugging in Britain was constructed as a new crime that represented specific threats to society in the context of a particular historical 'conjuncture', arguing that the focus on this newly acute 'problem' worked to obscure what was really a crisis for institutionalised ideological power. As the police and the media targeted 'mugging', the problem was amplified in the public imagination and in reality, constituting a 'moral panic'. Similarly, in early media coverage of YouTube, stories exhibiting the characteristics of a moral panic drew on and amplified two interlocking strains of public anxiety: youth and morality on the one hand, and new media and its 'effects' on the other. Drotner (1999) describes this double pattern of convergence between new media anxiety and moral anxiety as a 'media panic', and demonstrates that it has a long history as an 'intrinsic and recurrent' feature of modernity.

Tom Rawstorne and Brad Crouch's (2006) opinion piece in the Murdoch-owned, News Limited paper *The Sunday Mail* provided a telling early example, by turns blaming and absolving both young people and YouTube for social deviance. Rawstorne and Crouch (2006) painted YouTube as a video free-for-all, experiencing 'unchecked growth' where a sinister space filled with graphic content lies only a few mouse-clicks behind 'music videos, general entertainment . . . or just people mucking around with a video camera'. YouTube, they suggested, provided a platform for exhibitionists, beyond the reach of Australian media regulators because of the international nature of the Internet. Young people were framed as both agents and victims – responsible for the majority of YouTube's mundane content (teenage hijinks and bedroom lip synching) and much of its hypermediated hooliganism (car surfing, happy-slapping, public vandalism, and school-yard brawls), but also as a vulnerable group at risk from exposure to footage of Hitler's speeches, racist propaganda, gruesome autopsies, dismemberment footage, and videos of mortar attacks in Baghdad.

This media panic convergence is exemplified by stories about the then-new concept of 'cyberbullying' – the use of digital technologies to bully others, especially by posting humiliating or insulting videos, or by using video to document and celebrate acts of violence. In March 2007, the Victorian Government in Australia blocked access to YouTube from school property in part as a response to the uploading of a video showing twelve boys sexually abusing a seventeen-year-old Victorian girl (Smith, 2007). Similar calls to restrict access to the website to combat cyberbullying came from teachers' groups and school boards in the UK ('Teachers in websites closure call', 2007) and the US (Kranz, 2008). In response, YouTube launched its own anti-cyberbullying initiative – the Beatbullying channel, which no longer exists ('YouTube tackles bullying online', 2007). This new category of cyberbullying, which academia had been complicit in creating (see, for example, Patchin and Hinduja, 2006; Slonje and Smith, 2008), is a good illustration of how moral panics around youth, violence, and risk can be linked to existing media effects discourses, producing a media panic (Drotner, 1999).

The media discourses around issues of morality in YouTube, the tone of alarm in Rawstorne and Crouch's 2,000-word demonisation of the site, and the construction of the new category of 'cyberbullying', can be seen as symptoms of uneasiness and uncertainty around media expertise and moral authority provoked by the uses of digital media technologies such as mobile phones and the Internet for self-publishing. These moral panics were further amplified by the utopian hyperbole about 'Web 2.0' and the democratisation of cultural production, because they could simply invert the value judgements without disturbing the assumptions underlying the trope of a user-led 'revolution'. It is the same myth of mass democratisation as a direct effect of technological change that underpinned both *TIME Magazine*'s announcement that the 'Person of the Year' for 2006 was 'You' (Grossman, 2006b) and Andrew Keen's (2007) *The Cult of the Amateur*, which launched a polemical assault on participatory online culture on the grounds that it was eroding intellectual expertise and moral standards (35–46).

The themes of these stories about early YouTube are not new. They fit a pattern of rhetoric around the mass popularisation of new media technologies and forms that has been around since early modernity. Concerns emerged around the pauper press in the early nineteenth century (Hartley, 2008b) and the emergence of the portable hand camera at the beginning of the twentieth (Mensel, 1991; Seiberling and Bloore, 1986; Nead, 2004), reproducing similar anxieties about the tools of cultural production or cultural record being in the hands of the masses – or more specifically, the 'children of the lower classes' (Springhall, 1999). Further, the mobilisation of moral panic discourses has been business-as-usual for the media for decades when dealing with topics like new media, youth, and violence (see McRobbie and Thornton, 2002) – the discourse of the moral panic is now simply part of the professional repertoire of journalists, and many ordinary news consumers are able to recognise and critique it as well, so that 'moral panic' is simply part of the repertoire of reporting itself. But, as Driscoll and Gregg (2008) note, one important point of difference in contemporary moral panics, particularly about the Internet, is that the 'establishment' discourses, as represented by the mainstream media, are less hegemonic than they were in earlier periods, and therefore less able really to contain the debates. Rather, they necessarily incorporate a wide range of dissenting views precisely because the web makes it possible to publicise a range of opinions; and in 2017, media hegemony is radically distributed, so that 'the media' has no clear moral centre. For example, the social media hashtag campaign #metoo, which women all over the world used in October 2017 to disclose experiences of sexual harassment and assault, was framed as a social media-fuelled 'moral panic about men' by the left-libertarian publication *Spiked Online* (Whelan, 2017).

This is not to say that there are no risks or antisocial behaviours associated with YouTube – far from it (and the challenges with platform governance are discussed in Chapters 4, 5, and 6). But the assumption that digital media technologies directly cause antisocial phenomena and that users (especially young users) of these technologies are passive victims is unhelpful to addressing the issues at hand. Further, YouTubers them-selves are highly invested participants in media debates about YouTube's value, risk, and benefits, and, as we discuss in later chapters, they are very active in contesting and co-developing behavioural norms for the communities in which they under-stand themselves to be participants. These ethical aspects of participation in YouTube cannot be understood without a situated understanding of the platform's cultures of use and its diverse and varied community norms. In YouTube, these norms are continually being co-created, contested, and negoti-ated in the YouTube 'community' and across social media, as discussed in Chapter 4.

## YouTube and Celebrity Culture

A common assumption underlying the most celebratory accounts of the democratisation of cultural production in the mid 2000s (Grossman, 2006a, 2006b) was that raw talent combined with digital distribution could convert directly to legitimate success and media fame – if only the right platform were provided. This assumption was especially noticeable in the early mainstream media discourse around amateur video, usually invoking individual success stories that appear to real-ise this promise. For example, early in YouTube's history, the media interest in 'Lazy Sunday' turned the mainstream media spotlight on comedian and actor Andy Samberg, at the time a little-known new cast-member of *Saturday Night Live*. Samberg and his writing partners Jorma Taccone and Akiva Schnaffer came to the attention of the entertainment industry after posting their sketch comedy to the video-sharing website Channel101.com, which runs monthly screenings of user-created film, and on their own website The Lonely Island (Stein, 2006), which was still in operation in 2017.[2] The suc-cess of their videos on these sites, especially *The 'Bu* (short for 'Malibu'), their parody of US teen drama *The O.C.*, brought the team to the notice of Fox executives, who commissioned a pilot for a sketch comedy series (titled *Awesometown*). Though this series was not picked up, it did score the team a job writing for MTV, eventually landing them both in front of and behind the *Saturday Night Live* cameras.

In another success story, home-made music videos featuring US band *OK Go* dancing on treadmills and in their backyard pushed the band into the mainstream after fans took the videos from the band's official website and uploaded them to YouTube (Adegoke, 2006). Similarly, musician Terra Naomi secured a recording contract after becoming one of the most subscribed artists on YouTube musician's channel (Adegoke 2006; Hutchinson, 2007). And Justin Bieber – once responsible for the most-viewed video on the platform – was reportedly discovered in 2008 by a talent scout who came across videos of him busking that had been uploaded to the site. As recording labels and talent scouts increasingly turned their attention to online publishing opportunities (Bruno, 2007), even in its first few years YouTube had been mythologised as a way to 'broadcast yourself' into fame and fortune.

In 2003, when reality TV was still in its heyday, Nick Couldry argued that, in the mainstream media, the distance between 'ordinary' citizen and celebrity could only be bridged when the ordinary person gained access to the modes of representation of the mass media, making the transition from what Couldry called 'ordinary worlds' to 'media worlds'. For Couldry, rather than blurring distinctions between the ordinary person and the celebrity, rags-to-riches stories and Reality TV alike *reproduced* the distinctions between the 'media world' and the 'ordinary world', which 'disguises (and therefore helps naturalise) the inequality of symbolic power which media institutions represent' (2000: 16). The promise that talented but undiscovered YouTubers could make the leap from their 'ordinary worlds' to the bona fide 'media world' was firmly embedded in YouTube itself, evident in a number of YouTube's talent discovery competitions and initiatives. In response to the success of OK Go, YouTube created a dedicated channel for musicians, to which 120,000 signed up in the three months between June 2006 (when the service was launched) and August 2006 (Adegoke, 2006). Promotions to encourage the creation of quality DIY content included the 'My Grammy Moment' competition, where YouTube musicians performed versions of the Foo Fighters' song 'The Pretender' on their chosen instruments in a bid to win a spot performing live with the band at the Grammy awards ceremony;[3] various short film competitions, including the first 'International Film Competition' in November 2007; the 'From Here to Awesome' contest in February 2008;[4] and the 'sketchies' comedy awards. In 2008 and 2009 the site partnered with the London Symphony Orchestra to create an orchestra through online collaboration. Participants were selected from users who had submitted two audition videos, put through a judging process, and then eventually voted upon by the YouTube community. The winners were brought together to play a show at Carnegie Hall, and content from the performance, auditions, practice, and performance was uploaded to the site. The event was repeated again in 2010–11.

Despite appearances, these examples do not in themselves realise the myth of DIY celebrity so much as they demonstrate its limits. In Graeme Turner's (2004; 2006) discussion of the topic – in part a response to John Hartley's (1999) discussion of the democratisation of the media and the development of Do-It-Yourself citizenship – he argues that the increased representation of ordinary people as potential or temporary celebrities in the mass media represents the 'demoticisation' rather than the 'democratisation' of the media. Even when ordinary people become celebrities through their own creative efforts, there is no necessary transfer of media power: they remain within the *system* of celebrity native to, and controlled by, the media industries (whether the Hollywood film system or tabloid TV). For Turner, the 'demotic turn' in media culture relies on the existing structures of celebrity to deliver 'ordinary celebrity', which, far from providing alternatives to the existing media industry, is produced and captured by it.

In its early period, YouTube did open up possibilities for the commercialisation of amateur content, and in some cases turned the producers of that content into celebrities. But, as the examples discussed above show, the residual logics of traditional media industries had a persistent influence, whereby the marker of success for these new forms, para-doxically, was not so much their online popularity but their subsequent ability to pass through the gate-keeping mecha-nisms of old media – the recording contract, the film festival, the television pilot, the advertising deal.

By 2017, the star and brand power of YouTubers had dra-matically and exponentially increased and the media ecology had transformed more generally, but the 'fame' narrative remained. YouTubers are newsworthy when they themselves do something that brings them notoriety or an attention spike, but also when they are picked up as guests on Ellen DeGeneres's talk show *Ellen* (which regularly 'discovers' viral talent through vernacular video), or when their web series or videoblog gets picked up for development by streaming screen providers like Netflix. Reporting on these developments, of course, is one of the ways that mainstream media reinforces its own cultural power, as well as maintaining relevance to the market.

While popular content on YouTube has always come from a variety of sources, including the mainstream media and the music industry, YouTube gradually developed and then commercialised its own, internal, system of celebrity based on and reflecting the vernacular conventions and values of its various platform cultures. From the beginning, there were YouTube celebrities. Some of them were famous for being infamous, the targets of trolls, or because they were consid-ered obnoxious, or annoying: Chris Crocker of 'Leave Britney Alone!' fame[5] would certainly be one. But however spectacu-larly bizarre his performances may have seemed, Crocker's

fairly lengthy tenure as a 'star' YouTuber (he deleted his channel, citing problems with toxic commenters, in 2015) could
only be achieved by ongoing participation *in* YouTube. This
is quite different from the short-term flare of attention a *Big
Brother* contestant once received at the whim of a television
producer, or indeed the kind of celebrity associated with
one-off viral videos that give the creators of the videos (or
their subjects) their fabled fifteen minutes of fame. Earlier
(Burgess and Green, 2008), we traced the emergence of new
forms of commercial, professionalising content creators who
were capitalising on YouTube's vernacular, platform-specific
cultural practices. We called these home-grown stars 'entrepreneurial vloggers'. They might not have been behaving
like traditional media professionals, but they were definitely
operating with commercial intent. They were already making
a living via advertising revenue, reaching large audiences with
content produced within and for YouTube, often with their
own external websites as well. Some of our examples were
whatthebuck (Michael Buckley, who vlogged about popular
events and celebrities), hotforwords (Marlina Orlova, who
specialised in sexy infotainment with a focus on etymology)
and sxephil (Philip DeFranco, who had a fast-paced, often
satirical news vlog). While Orlova's fame has passed its peak,
both Buckley and DeFranco were still highly active and successful YouTubers and cross-platform media professionals
by the end of 2017. They are not tabloid celebrities; rather,
they were among the first *stars* of an emergent media system,
with distinctive YouTube 'acts', consistent personae, and high
levels of expertise at engaging YouTube audiences through
the specific affordances of the platform. They became famous
not for being famous but for doing something in particular
very well. That 'something' was at first glance scrappy and
amateurish and unlikely to accrue prestige in the traditional
media or arts industries – but, it turns out, it is exactly what
is required to build a successful media brand centred around
YouTube.

Over the past decade, lucrative but precarious careers have been built on just these kinds of carefully produced and platform-specific cultural forms and practices, from comedy news to gameplay to cooking shows and beauty vlogging, giving rise to the new 'influencer' (Abidin, 2015a; 2015b; Duffy, 2017) and 'social media entertainment' (Cunningham et al., 2016) sub-sectors of the creative industries. Their business models may also involve complex relationships to brands and marketing, most famously in beauty but also in automotive, alcohol, toys, and snackfoods (Nazerali, 2017). As industry insiders make clear, influencers are not the same as traditional media celebrities, and neither are the star YouTubers. These content creators are embedded in the cultural economy of digital media, organically engaged with its vernacular culture, and exhibit mastery of its aesthetic and communicative codes. Successful YouTubers know how to articulate authenticity to entertainment and to navigate the inherent ambivalence of their performance and self-representations – using combinations of intimacy, humour, and irreverence, carefully balancing authenticity, community, and brand relationships (for further detailed discussions of these cultural and economy dynamics, see Banet-Weiser, 2012; Duffy, 2017; Smith, 2014).

In 2017, any rise to success that YouTubers experience is still persistently represented in traditional media outlets as being all the more remarkable given the mundane, tasteless, or talentless qualities of the amateur video which is still represented as making up the bulk of user-created content on YouTube. In a segment on YouTube from the ABC (US) Network's *20/20* that aired very early on in the platform's life, journalist John Stossel covered the perceived cultural range of amateur video, affecting a somewhat typical tone of incredulity in his opening address to the audience:

> Do you like watching kids doing stupid and reckless things? Animals doing cute things?

Beauty queens falling down?
Or a thousand prisoners dancing to the music of Thriller?
It's all on YouTube.

Although YouTube has become a mainstream source of commercial online video content, the mythology of the accidental,
'viral' video star still persists; and it is a myth that is carefully
cultivated by successful YouTubers and by the platform itself
(featuring 'accidental' YouTube stars that were the subjects of
viral videos heavily in each of its birthday specials).

At the same time, viral videos or memes can fail to reward
their original creators, putting money in other people's pock-
ets; or they can exploit or humiliate their subjects. A good
example here is the not always willing or aware stars of viral
videos and memes, who become famous through the rapid
and extensive spread of content featuring them. There are
issues of exploitation as much as empowerment at work here
(Senft, 2013: 352–3), where videosharing can expose strangers
to unasked-for fame – or even ridicule – without their con-
sent. There is rising awareness, too, of the complexity around
microcelebrity for, and even the commercial exploitation of,
children who are turned into 'micro-microcelebrities' via their
parents' YouTube channels (Abidin, 2015a); their unwanted
fame can sometimes follow them into adolescence and even
adulthood.

## The Changing Meanings of Vernacular Video

Many of YouTube's vernacular forms pre-existed YouTube
and even the web, having historical continuities with collective and collaborative alternative media subcultures whose
activities pre-existed but were available to prime the platform
with content and practices outside the limited cultural imagination of the founders, as Henry Jenkins' (2009) essay in
the earlier edition of this book showed. Jenkins argued that
alternative media, zine culture, fan vidders, and activist video

cultures 'paved the way for the early embrace, quick adoption, and diverse use of [platforms like YouTube]' (Jenkins, 2009).

Much of the content posted on YouTube has always been very ordinary, mundane, and personal. A Pew Internet and American Life article published in 2015 for YouTube's tenth birthday highlighted the fact that, despite the disproportionately large audiences for a very few star YouTubers, of the 31 per cent of online adults who posted a video to a website in 2013 (a figure which had more than doubled since 2009), 45 per cent uploaded 'their own video of a pet or animal', 58 per cent posted a video showing 'friends and family doing everyday things', 56 per cent posted a video 'of themselves or others doing funny things', 54 per cent posted a video 'of an event they attended', while fewer had posted 'tutorial videos' (30%) or 'intentionally staged or scripted videos' (23%) – and, tellingly, only a third of them said they uploaded a video 'in the hope that it would be widely viewed or "go viral"' (Anderson, 2015). Through the theoretical lens of 'vernacular creativity' (Burgess, 2006), which incorporates mundane practices like everyday storytelling, home movies (Zimmermann, 1995), and personal photography, the creation and sharing of videos can be seen as a means of collective cultural participation, social connection, and everyday aesthetic experimentation as well as a mode of individual self-expression that is not always primarily motivated by the desire for individual attention from a large audience.

The 'vlog' (short for videoblog) genre is one of YouTube's most central cultural forms, underpinning many of the platform's most popular channels, as well as being extremely prevalent form of originally 'amateur' video and vernacular creativity in YouTube from the early years of the platform through to 2017. It is also a genre that predates the platform – see especially Theresa Senft's (2008) discussion of the camgirls' authentic, 'ordinary' mode of address and socially networked practices of audience engagement, as well as Trine Bjørkman Berry's (2015) cultural history of videoblogging, revealing it as a project that precedes YouTube by many years. In their most basic form, typically structured primarily around a monologue delivered directly to camera, vlogs were often produced with little more than a webcam and some witty editing, with subject matter ranging from comedy to celebrity gossip and reasoned political debate through to the mundane details of everyday life; but good storytelling and a direct, personal address have always been essential to the genre.

One of the early viral hits of YouTube, the 'Hey' clip,[6] illustrated both the mainstream media perspective on YouTube – the articulation of youth, gender, and DIY celebrity – and the vernacular creativity perspective, where, through digital media platforms, formerly private media consumption and cultural production were being remediated as part of the cultural public sphere. In the video, Israeli twenty-somethings Lital Mizel and her friend Adi Frimerman lip-sync, dance, play air guitar, and generally goof around to the Pixies song 'Hey'. The video was clearly shot in several takes, and has undergone extensive editing so that each cut is precisely in time with the beat of the song. It had had several million views by mid 2006, remained popular on the website, and had received more than 34 million views by September 2017. Demonstrating a sophisticated understanding of the rules of the vernacular genre she was drawing on – the bedroom dance video – as well as a self-deprecating awareness of its status *as* a vernacular form, Mizel explained the motivation and meaning behind the video:

> We just turned on the camera and danced funny . . . I keep asking people why do you like it, and they say, 'Because it's reality.' You see it's homemade, that we're so spontaneous and natural – dancing, having fun. It makes people remember when they were young and danced in front of the mirror. (Kornblum, 2006)[7]

The clip, which has somehow avoided takedown for copyright violation, has become iconic in digital culture, garnering a steady stream of mostly positive (and, more recently, nostalgic) comments. While the clip didn't convert into ongoing fame or professionalisation as YouTubers, Mizel maintains an active channel on YouTube with just under 10,000 subscribers as at September 2017, where she posts videoblogs and remixed music videos. In 2014, drawing on the education in film-making they had acquired in the intervening years, and after reportedly securing a meeting with the band when they were touring Israel, Mizel and Frimerman were given the job of directing an official Pixies video (Gorali, 2014), thereby successfully leveraging the ongoing fame garnered through their one viral hit. They completed the project and appeared on camera – dancing with abandon at a forest rave – in the music video for the Pixies single 'Ring the Bell'.[8]

The original 'Hey' clip, along with the many thousands of other lip-sync or cover song videos like it, was both an example and a witty and self-aware celebration of the mediatised 'bedroom cultures' of young people, particularly girls. Productive play, media consumption, and cultural performance have always been part of the repertoire of these semi-private spaces of cultural participation (McRobbie and Garber, 1976; Baker, 2004), but in the 1990s and 2000s they became increasingly publicised via webcams, social media, and YouTube itself. These platforms for public performance and audience engagement added new dimensions to these circuits of what had been relatively 'privatized media use' (Bovill and Livingstone, 2001).

Webcam cultures – also associated with the online cultures of women and girls – had a significant history before YouTube, and early academic research and critique noted the implications of webcam culture for surveillance, shifting it from a vertical to a horizontal or 'participatory' model (Knight, 2000). In contrast to the self-exploitative mode of participation in Reality TV (Andrejevic, 2003), these authors argued that 'cam-girls' had greater control over the conditions of both production and consumption of their own representations, so that webcam cultures should be understood at least as much in terms of 'empowering exhibitionism' (Koskela, 2004) as voyeurism. Like vlogging and selfie cultures, early webcam cultures could therefore be understood as a means to social connection and community, as Theresa M. Senft argued in her pioneering book *Camgirls* (2008), in which she also coined the term 'microcelebrity'.

As with the 'moral' dimensions of participatory culture discussed earlier in this chapter, tensions between 'expression' and 'exhibitionism', performance and surveillance are actively negotiated by the participants themselves. Even at the beginning, YouTube's vernacular producers attempted to control the 'publicness' of their participation in various ways, albeit with varying degrees of awareness of the extent to which relatively 'private' contributions might be accessed in ways outside of their control (Lange, 2007b). In 2017, the more prominent participants in videoblogging, whether amateur or professional, cannot help but be aware of discourses of narcissism and microcelebrity because they have been so heavily featured in media commentary; and the boundaries of these norms are reflexively negotiated by videobloggers as well as their audiences.

The case of Lonelygirl15 (Bakioğlu, 2016) was an early example of the complex new relations between 'amateur' and 'professional' cultural production, the emergence of platform-centred vernacular codes and conventions, the challenges with controlling brands in an era of 'spreadable media' (Jenkins et al., 2013), and, most importantly, the slipperiness of authenticity in YouTube. Between July and September 2006, mainstream US media outlets such as *The New York Times*, *The Los Angeles Times*, and *The San Francisco Chronicle* became particularly enamoured with Bree, a YouTuber videoblogging under the username Lonelygirl15. Her emotional post on 4 July 2006 discussing how troubles with her parents were getting in the way of a burgeoning relationship drew half a million views in forty-eight hours, a significant increase from the 50,000 to 100,000 views a week her previous videos had received (Davis, 2006: 238). Lonelygirl15's videos were impassioned – they described a fraught relationship with her religious parents and played out the quandaries and capriciousness of her relationship with friend and fellow vlogger Daniel. Lonelygirl15's posts eventually developed a stable viewership of around 300,000 views each.

Media commentators, especially *New York Times* blogger Virginia Heffernan,[9] took an interest in the rapid fame of Bree, as well as the high level of speculation building in YouTube's user community regarding the authenticity of her videos. Though they fit the vlogging mould – a talking head speaking straight-to-camera, and covered the domestic, personal politics considered characteristic of the form, some of them looked 'too slick'. They were a little too well edited, and revealed a series of events that unfolded a little too much like a narrative for a personal journal.

The YouTube community was especially curious about these videos. Users began openly to query their authenticity in comments on YouTube, in online discussion, and in replies to blog posts. The press joined the discussion. Some guardedly discussed Lonelygirl15 and acknowledged the debate about whether Bree was a real vlogger while at the same time using her videos as an example to explore the creative capacities of young people (Murphy, 2006). Others, however, jumped headlong into the debate about her legitimacy (Chonin, 2006), especially once the truth was revealed: that the Lonelygirl15 'vlog' was really a film-making experiment by independent producers Mesh Flinders, Miles Beckett, and Greg Goodfried (Fine, 2006; Gentile, 2006; Heffernan and Zeller, 2006).

The case of Lonelygirl15 both supported and subverted the mythologies around the significance of YouTube's amateur content. Skilfully appropriating the aesthetics and formal constraints of the vlog and its confessional style, the Lonelygirl videos publicised and legitimised vlogging as a genre of cultural production. Arguably, however, it was the embeddedness within YouTube's social network of each character in the Lonelygirl15 universe that marked the videos as authentic: characters in the series used their own YouTube profiles and videos to introduce themselves and carry the narrative, as well as forging connections across other social media platforms such as MySpace. Bree, Daniel, and other characters were made real not only through the skills of writers and actors, but also through their apparent use of YouTube to create and negotiate social relationships with other participants in the social network. Similarly, the 'gotcha' energies generated by Lonelygirl15 – the discussion around the authenticity of the characters and the series and the investigative efforts of YouTube users – point to the centrality of these social networking functions.

Lonelygirl15 violated the ideology of authenticity associated with DIY culture, while at the same time being wholly consistent with the way early YouTube actually worked. Though the series continued after the ruse was revealed, expanding beyond the bedroom locations to adopt something more of a cinema verité style, Lonelygirl15 introduced new possibilities for experimenting with and expanding the uses of the vlog form within YouTube, and marked a new phase of ambivalence with respect to authenticity, intimacy, and branding in videoblogging culture. Authenticity (even when it is performed reflexively or ironically) has remained a fundamental cultural logic of YouTube. Irresolvable, dynamic relationships between authenticity, intimacy, and community produce the YouTubeness of YouTube, distinguishing it from mainstream media, but generating ambivalence in the context of a brand-saturated commercial culture, which all YouTubers need to navigate (Banet-Weiser, 2012; Cunningham and Craig, 2017). Negotiating the ambivalence of authenticity and performing it anyway is therefore an essential competency of successful YouTubers and social media influencers.

## The Copyright Wars

As YouTube's relationships with the incumbent media and music industries have evolved, copyright has been a particularly fraught area; and YouTube's solutions to the copyright problem have helped shape and constrain its culture. Particularly in the lead-up to Google's acquisition of the company, discussion on the technology and business pages pointed to the presence of copyright-infringing content on YouTube as a possible encumbrance to the sale or to the expansion of YouTube's content offerings (Bawden and Sabbagh, 2006; Elias, 2006; Goo, 2006; Harris, 2006; Kopytoff, 2006; McKenna, 2006). Early reporting about YouTube around the issue of copyright reproduced the mythology of YouTube as disruptive upstart in a David-and-Goliath relationship with big media. We saw stories about the sabre-rattling by big business and large rights holders threatening lawsuits, and concerned about YouTube as a sanctuary for, or even a business built upon, copyright infringement (Blakely, 2007; Elfman, 2006; Karnitschnig and Delaney, 2006; Martinson, 2006). Reporting concerned with 'hard' technological innovation as YouTube began to develop various Digital Rights Management strategies and other copyright controls made up a second group (Geist, 2006; Letzing, 2007; Swartz, 2007; Veiga, 2006). And we saw stories about YouTube's copyright management strategies, the lawsuits actually levelled, the deals done, and the videos removed, reported because they were connected to the always-looming avalanche of lawsuits that might, at any moment, bring the company to its knees (Arthur, 2006; Charny, 2007; Li, 2006; Noguchi and Goo, 2006).

As the success of 'Lazy Sunday' brought the service to public attention and the potential of the platform as a way to launch viral successes became accepted,[10] large media companies including both NBC and Viacom began a cautious embrace of the service as a promotional platform (*PC Magazine*, 2006).

In March 2006, after the removal of the 'Lazy Sunday' video proved YouTube to be 'trustworthy partners' in the eyes of NBC Universal's Chief Executive Jeff Zucker (Ryan, 2006), NBC was attempting to straighten out a deal to deliver clips of NBC content via the service. By 23 October 2007, however, talks had soured and NBC had moved all its content to 'private' status as it launched testing of its own premium content website Hulu.[11] Offering television programing and some films from the NBC Universal and Fox stables, media hype circulating around Hulu positioned it as a direct competitor to YouTube, delivering content and allowing users to embed clips from the service into their own webpages.

Not long after the removal of 'Lazy Sunday', US media conglomerate Viacom filed a lawsuit against YouTube and Google claiming $1 billion for copyright infringement (Hilderbrand, 2007). This followed a demand in late 2006 that the service remove more than 100,000 clips of Viacom content, including videos from Viacom brands Comedy Central, Nickelodeon, and MTV (Becker, 2007). Despite initially embracing YouTube – particularly for youth-culture-oriented channel MTV2 (Wallenstein, 2006b; Morrissey, 2006) – Viacom was less convinced by the end of 2006 of the promotional value of having videos on the service. Claiming programs such as Comedy Central's *The Daily Show* were among the most viewed videos on the website, and unhappy with the revenue-sharing deal they could negotiate, Viacom accused YouTube of unduly profiting from their labour.[12] 'YouTube and Google retain all of the revenue generated from [users uploading videos]', the company claimed, 'without extending fair compensation to the people who have expended all of the effort and cost to create it' (Karnitschnig, 2007). As YouTube was already selling advertising on some videos across the site, and didn't police closely enough for Viacom's liking the uploading of copyrighted content without permission from copyright owners, Viacom argued that YouTube not only profited from but had legitimated the uploading of content that infringes upon the copyrights of Viacom and others. As the media conglomerate wrote in a press release shortly after filing their original motion:

> There is no question that YouTube and Google are continuing to take the fruit of our efforts without permission and destroying enormous value in the process. This is value that rightfully belongs to the writers, directors and talent who create it and companies like Viacom that have invested to make possible this innovation and creativity.[13]

Viacom was not alone; in mid 2008 Silvio Berlusconi's Mediaset took action against YouTube for 500 million euros (US$780 million) for copyright infringement, TF1, the largest French broadcaster, filed suit for 100 million euros ('UPDATE 2-Mediaset sues Google, YouTube; seeks $780 mln, 2008'), and the English Premier League announced action against YouTube for copyright infringement in 2007 ('Premier League to take action against YouTube, 2007').

Viacom's legal actions in 2008 were already out of step with the everyday practices of their own audiences, and appeared to misread the signs of future digital transformation in the media industry. Online distribution – both through direct peer-to-peer technologies and online video sharing – is held to be partly responsible for the early success of both *The Daily Show* and *The Colbert Report* (Goetz, 2005; Broersma, 2007). In fact, *The Colbert Report*'s Stephen Colbert had made extensive uses of YouTube up until that point, including encouraging fans to post remixed videos of his performances to the website. Colbert also gained both notice and notoriety when the US non-profit station C-SPAN demanded that a very popular clip of his performance at the 2006 White House Correspondents Dinner be removed, despite the fact that it was already freely available through the (then separate, and now defunct) Google Video service (Delaney, 2006). Beyond this incident, Viacom was at times clearly overzealous in patrolling YouTube, resulting in both legitimate parodies and completely unrelated videos being claimed by accident (Mills, 2007). Viacom, Google later charged, was uploading many of these clips to YouTube themselves, hiring multiple marketing agencies to use 'astroturfing' techniques to seed viral clips by uploading them from multiple computers under 'ordinary' usernames (YouTube Official Blog, 2010).

Viacom's principal interest was in proving that a significant proportion of the overall archive consisted of copyright-infringing content, and that this content was driving much of the audience engagement on the platform. But as we discuss in the next chapter, popularity for YouTube content at the time revolved as much around what was 'Most Discussed' or 'Most Responded' as it did what was 'Most Viewed'. It tended to be vernacular content, not traditional media content, that was most discussed or most responded; and the home-grown YouTubers who created that vernacular content dominated the most-subscribed channels list at the time. YouTube's value was created as much through vernacular content creation and related audience practices (of engagement, of sharing, and of curation of content) as it was through distributing pre-packaged media content. While the courts found in Google's favour in 2010 and, following a series of appeals, the case was settled out of court in 2014 (Kafka, 2014), copyright is the area of governance that has received the most attention by the platform, and the area where balancing the interests of the platform's various 'markets' (of content suppliers, audiences, advertisers, and media partners) is most complex and questionable in the fairness of its application.

YouTube's internal copyright policy, designed to comply with external frameworks, is managed through complex automation mechanisms like Content ID, which matches uploaded content against a database of copyrighted material. Such mechanisms are essential for maintaining the protections afforded to platforms under the Digital Millennium Copyright Act (DMCA), which provides a 'safe harbour' for such intermediaries who act in good faith to remove infringing content once they become aware of it. However, Content ID regularly flags non-infringing videos, (Solomon, 2015), the counter-flagging measures are rarely used; and most creators are unaware of their rights to reuse material, especially under Fair Use provisions (and their approximate equivalents in non-US jurisdictions) – with an overall chilling effect on creativity.

The doctrine of Fair Use is intended to reduce the burden on creators and allow them to build on each other's work, allowing them to reuse, remix, critique, and parody limited portions of other creators' work without the need to secure explicit permission (see Aufderheide and Jaszi, 2011). The YouTube Community Guidelines on copyright (YouTube, 2017a) do not proactively point users toward fair use provisions or their equivalents in non-US jurisdictions, saying simply 'don't upload videos you didn't make, or use content in your videos that someone else owns the copyright to, such as music tracks, snippets of copyrighted programs, or videos made by other users, without necessary authorizations'. While the more extensive Copyright Centre pages do mention Fair Use and the website provides detailed guidance on the subject (YouTube, 2017b), at first glance the message most certainly isn't overly encouraging:

> Make sure you understand how fair use and the public domain work before you choose to dispute for either of those reasons. YouTube can't help you determine whether you should dispute a claim. You may want to seek your own legal advice if you're not sure what to do.

> Disputes shouldn't be taken lightly, and are only intended for cases where you have all necessary rights to the content in your video. Repeated or malicious abuse of the dispute process can result in penalties against your video or channel.

The 'What is Fair Use' page (YouTube, 2017b) does state that the company asks rights-holders to confirm they have considered fair use before lodging a copyright takedown request (as is required by law), and have selected a small number of creators for a program showcasing best practice in fair use, even indemnifying the creators for up to $1 million of legal costs 'in the event the takedown results in a lawsuit for copyright infringement'. Predictably, the creators and content chosen for this program are highly legitimising – brief clips from a heavily criticised commercial used in a media critique; feminist remixes of *Twilight*; and political commentary using footage of opponents for the purposes of debates.

However accurate or fair the mechanisms, to police everyday reuses of media content as copyright infringement, framing them as piracy, is too simplistic a way to deal with the emergent audience practices and dynamics of 'spreadability' (Jenkins et al., 2013) and memetic culture (Burgess, 2008; Shifman, 2014) associated with digital media. As we discuss in the next chapter, YouTube's popular culture has long been characterised by its own 'native' genres (like vlogging), as well as by the clip and the quote – short grabs or edited selections of TV shows, music videos, or movies uploaded informally by ordinary users, and which are also material traces of everyday audience practices. Selecting and editing a particular moment from a favourite television show or sporting match is an example of what Fiske (1992b: 37–8) described as 'enunciative productivity'. Where these small portions of media content were shared by ordinary users, it was in a similar way to how GIFs are used on Facebook and Twitter – as visual annotations, reactions, and exclamations (Miltner and Highfield, 2017). As we have discussed elsewhere (Burgess, 2012a), it is these amateur reuses of media content in vernacular creations, like music videos – often created by young people as an organic part of their fandom – that have been treated particularly cruelly (on the 'Dancing Baby' case, see Rimmer, 2017). Copyright policing has significantly chilling effects on vernacular creativity and fan engagement.

On the other hand, creativity can come from even the most draconian constraints. Infamously, the most popular 'literal music videos' (including Total Eclipse of the Heart), which recast the lyrics of popular songs to literally represent the on-screen action from the more artsy end of the music video spectrum, were taken down for copyright. But there is also the 'musicless music videos' genre, which replaces the song audio with Foley effects and vocalisations in sync with the video's visual content. The musicless music video works both as cultural parody and evasion of the audio recognition built into Content ID – a meme born from copyright control (Sánchez-Olmos and Viñuela, 2017); but one which is in constant danger of takedown as it preserves the original music video's visuals.

Of course, the increased monetisation possibilities for 'amateur' content have complicated any simple division between vernacular or everyday uses and commercial or professional uses of content, placing amateur remixes, fan videos, and parodies at further risk. Amateur and viral videos that originated on YouTube can be highly commercialisable, and so copyright plays a role in protecting and rewarding non-corporate creators. For example, Morreale (2014) traces the career of the Annoying Orange character (an animated orange with recurring, antisocial mannerisms and a high, irritating voice) through the trajectory from viral amateur creation by a film student to television series and merchandise line, using it to construct a narrative about the professionalisation of YouTube (in this case, at least, rewarding the original creator).

Formalised copyright logics are an especially acute challenge to the vernacular meme cultures of YouTube. Memes are different from one-off, widely viewed viral videos (which may have a single creator) because they involve many different creators generating iterative variations on multiple combinations of 'original' ideas, also drawn from multiple sources (Burgess, 2008; Shifman, 2014). The features that make memes popular and creative also make it difficult (and counter-intuitive) to identify ownership of the ideas for the purposes of copyright enforcement. Things get even more difficult when commercially exploitable memes are themselves built on the borrowing, remixing, or appropriation of pre-existing folk or non-commercial popular culture. This issue becomes of particular relevance to instances where vernacular memes end up being captured by commercial interests through the use of copyright, without compensation for the collective creativity that originated, replicated, and created variations on amateur or vernacular cultural ideas from a range of sources. For example, Soha and McDowell (2016) discuss the case of the Harlem Shake – a meme in the form of an Internet dance craze whose variation and viral spread were the result of distributed vernacular contributions; but this popularity was captured via copyright control (enforced through Content ID) and exploited for profit by Bauer, the original producer of the EDM track to which the dance was set, which was only one element of the overall meme or 'craze', but the most easily exploitable through the logic of copyright.

It is difficult to avoid the sense of betrayal that YouTube's changing relationship to copyright has engendered. As Soha and McDowell put it:

> YouTube harnessed its ability to host copyrighted materials with limited legal liability into achieving market dominance and then harnessed its market dominance into the ability to force licensing on both content creators and copyright holders. (2016: 7)

This, the authors argue, is a betrayal of the '"basic bargain" of social and/or noncommercial culture exchange', setting up 'a pattern for increasingly aggressive for-profit harnessing of non-commercial and amateur cultural creation' and 'establishing a platform of aggressive digital sharecropping' (Soha and McDowell, 2016: 10).

Both user-uploaded traditional media content, then, and vernacular creativity (which also incorporates the reuse of commercial media content) have been value-building activities that were allowed to flourish in a relatively laissez-faire environment, but which have been increasingly subject to surveillance and control (including via automated and algorithmic means) as the business model has drifted into territory dominated by traditional media licensing. In the eyes of some critics this reduces YouTube's relationship with its user community to one of 'digital sharecropping'; on the other hand, YouTube's aspiring professional content creators need copyright to help them protect their precarious enterprises and careers from content theft and misappropriation by other users. Either way, the abuse and unevenness of access to the protections supposedly afforded to creators by copyright is still a fraught one, and its imbalance remains one of the key risks to supporting and maintaining a generative, participatory culture on the platform. Copyright remains at the centre of industry struggles for power and control, and plays a role in YouTube's cultural and intra-community politics as well, as discussed further in Chapters 4 and 5.

## YouTube  Mainstream Media

Amanda Lotz's book *The Television Will be Revolutionized* (first published in 2007) was one of the very first to deal with YouTube specifically. Her discussions of YouTube were evidently something of a late addition to the book, which was completed in late 2006, when YouTube was still a start-up, and it was only just beginning to receive a great deal of attention in the press and academia. On the implications of the proliferation of amateur video for industry production, cutting into demand, Lotz wrote:

> By late 2006, it remained unclear whether the flurry of amateur video was merely a passing trend or likely to revolutionize television [. . .] Like so much of the new technological space, existing amateur video was largely confined to the efforts of high-school and college-aged students by the end of 2006. But as cultural discussion of YouTube grew, politicians and corporations quickly began adding their videos, creating an odd amalgamation spanning talking-head video

> of Ted Kennedy, Paris Hilton's music video debut, and cats using human toilets. (Lotz, 2007: 252)

We see here, in the absence at the time of scholarly work on YouTube as a cultural system, the use of a list of oddities to signify the diversity of YouTube. We also see the speed at which YouTube has continued to grow and the way that, even in the space of twelve months, it had become normalised as part of the media environment. This is a pattern also borne out by the evolution of mainstream media discourse around YouTube – from oddity to the centre of serious industrial, legal, and moral issues.

By 2015, TIME was no longer saying that the person of the year was 'you'. Instead, they were saying that a decade of YouTube had 'changed the future of television' (Moylan, 2015) – not only by shifting how and where it is consumed and giving 'ordinary' people access to production, but by changing how it works as an industry, and the kinds of media forms, genres, and practices that constitute it. The article points, for example, to how YouTube has become integral to the success of TV shows as a supplementary or transmedia platform, and has enabled the emergence of 'a new crop of stars' whose success rests on their mastery of vernacular YouTube genres: PewDiePie (gameplay), Tyler Oakley (vlogging), and Bethany Mota ('haul videos'); as well as functioning as an archive *for* vintage and contemporary television – all aspects of the platform's culture that we discuss in later chapters. In the conclusion to the *Time* piece, YouTube's vernacular DNA was still on show and the mainstream media's hype of its revolutionary potential was still there, but its relationship to television in particular had been reconfigured:

> Rather than pirating off and siphoning from television, YouTube serves to amplify it, cultivating our remembrance and interest, giving us reasons to tune in – where would John Oliver be without all the YouTube clips? – and creating ideas for future shows. YouTube has not only replaced

public access television, a place where anyone could have a voice, but has perfected it, creating its own ecosystem that is a parallel to television. And these days, with teens thinking YouTube stars are bigger celebrities than the cast of the *Big Bang Theory*, it's only a matter of time before public access takes over all the airwaves.

YouTube is now mainstream media; but the media business is complex and rapidly changing. On the platform, user profiles have for some time been referred to as 'channels' (although many of the longest-running channels are still known by the individual pseudonymous usernames chosen by the early YouTubers). YouTube has experimented (often simultaneously) with a plethora of advertising models – from pre-rolls to in-display ads to channel sponsorships. Brand associations with popular YouTubers and cross-platform 'influencers' are a burgeoning part of the 'social media marketing' industry (Serazio and Duffy, 2017). The YouTube Partner Program, which allows creators to share in advertising revenue generated by views on their videos, was launched in April 2007 (YouTube Creator Blog, 2017). At first the program was invite only, then opened to all users from the 20 countries where the program was available in 2012 (Schroeder, 2012). Another five years later, in April 2017, in an effort to address mounting issues with problematic content, YouTube announced that creators could only turn on monetisation once they hit 10,000 lifetime views (YouTube Creator Blog, 2017) and went through a review process. The controversies around monetisation and demonetisation from the creator community's perspective are discussed further in Chapter 6.

YouTube has also been the site of new forms of intermediation and disintermediation in the digital media industry. It has seen the rise of a class of new digital intermediaries, the Multichannel Networks (MCNs) (Lobato, 2016; Cunningham et al., 2016). With their origins in the need to find a way to manage the 'messy middle' between advertisers and YouTube's chaotic content universe, in 2007 Google began to partner with external companies to 'aggregate ad sales across the platform, increase the quality of uploaded videos, reduce intellectual property infringements and generally make it a more appealing space for advertisers' (Lobato, 2016: 350–1). Since then, independent MCNs have rushed to exploit this middle zone of the digital media industries. While the business models of MCNs are varied, similarly to contemporary record labels or talent agencies, most MCNs aggregate similar YouTube channels within clearly defined market niches (like games, lifestyle and beauty, or how-to), provide sophisticated cross-platform metrics, and connect entrepreneurial YouTubers to brand sponsors for integrated advertising, additional content distribution and windowing strategies, and ancillary revenue and brand-building opportunities (like book publishing, live tours, and merchandising) – but unlike traditional record labels or talent agencies, sign-up is often managed online via click-through service agreements (Lobato, 2016: 355). Early MCNs that predated YouTube's move to aggregate channels were Machinima (for games) and Maker Studios (representing thousands of YouTube channels). By 2017, there were so many MCNs that YouTube metrics provider Socialblade (which in turn has a partnership with MCN BroadbandTV) was dedicating a section of its site to providing dynamic rankings of the top 250 networks.[14]

This middle coordination layer of YouTube's multi-sided market is volatile (Cunningham et al., 2016). Competition for social media talent is fierce, and MCNs have been both the instigators and targets of corporate acquisitions. Ultimately, it is the content creators who hold the key to the audience engagement and subscriber loyalty that the whole business is built on. Consequently, Cunningham et al. (2016) identify not only media production but also media management as a 'precarious' form of creative work. This precariousness, they argue, 'arises from the MCNs being creations of the volatile conditions within the new screen ecology; its accelerated evolution bears directly on their sustainability' (383). Ramon

Lobato (2016) draws out the cultural consequences of this extra layer of intermediation, arguing that 'it has entrenched entrepreneurial calculation as a cultural norm across the platform and it has further exposed YouTube's producer community to a range of digital economy discourses and expectations' (357). Further, because MCNs are primarily interested in channels that align with existing consumer 'verticals' (like fashion, beauty, games, and technology reviews), 'the rise of MCNs may start to have a visible effect on the generic make-up of the YouTube archive, by stimulating the production of certain kinds of content over others', and demoting more mundane or public interest-oriented content in the platform's attention economy (357–8).

While by 2017 YouTube was a dominant part of the multi-platform digital media industry with revenues reportedly in the billions of US dollars, as recently as 2016 the company still hadn't become profitable. At that time, YouTube CEO Susan Wojcicki was quoted as saying that profitability was not the highest priority for the company, which was 'still in investment mode' (Rao, 2016), indicating the importance of the platform's cultural discovery and experimentation function as well as the complexity of the business it is in. In 2017 the *LA Times* reported that YouTube advertising revenue (estimated at $10 billion and growing) was crucial to parent company Google/Alphabet, providing leverage for YouTube to license cable offerings for its fledgling YouTube TV initiative, and perhaps even cross-subsidising Alphabet's diversification into new areas like autonomous vehicles. Undoubtedly YouTube's vast archive of video content and interaction data is also an asset to Google's artificial intelligence research and development areas.

In the landscape of online video, new business models, new capacities for high-end video streaming, and ever-more accessible tools of production, editing, and audience engagement have continuously generated new and uncertain articulations between the digital technology business, social or community-driven media, and the mainstream commercial media industries. These uncertainties could partly explain the oscillation between two dominant explanatory frameworks for the platform – YouTube as a player in the digital economy on the one hand (the top-down view), and YouTube as a site of vernacular creativity and cultural chaos on the other (the bottom-up view).

But this 'top-down' versus 'bottom-up' perspective doesn't explain the career of YouTube as a platform. It is more helpful to understand YouTube as occupying an evolving institutional function – operating as a coordinating mechanism between individual and collective creativity and meaning production; and as a mediator among various competing industry, community, and audience interests – including its own. Over time, the coordination of and competition among these interests has contributed to the production of new media genres, cultural practices, and professional identities. The following chapter provides a detailed breakdown of these new genres, practices, and identities, grounded in an empirical analysis of YouTube's most popular videos and content creators.

CHAPTER THREE

# YouTube's Popular Culture

This chapter analyses the results of a large-scale analysis of YouTube's most popular content as it was in 2007. It describes YouTube's early culture of use, and reflects on how it has changed over the next decade. In the following sections, we describe the study design and its limitations, and reflect on how the metrics that YouTube uses to measure popularity also end up shaping popularity. We then present and discuss the core findings of the study, including the breakdown of vernacular and professional media content, the role of different actors in the YouTube uploader ecosystem, the cultural dynamics of key YouTube genres, and finally, the importance of YouTube's more recent emphasis on channels and subscribers rather than audience engagement with individual videos.

The content survey was the empirical heart of the book in its original version, and many of the ideas and examples in later chapters were drawn from this study. We have not repeated the study for the new edition – not only because it would have been physically impossible due to fundamental changes in the YouTube platform and interface (for reasons discussed in further detail below in the 'Shaping Popularity' section), but also because we believe there is significant historical value in this record of early YouTube culture. However, we have updated the language and provided contemporary comparisons, so that a story emerges about how YouTube's popular culture has changed over time; including especially how certain vernacular genres and practices that were still emerging in 2007 later became an essential part of the platform's cultural logics, a phenomenon which was still clearly evident in 2017.

## Accounting for Popularity

When we designed the content survey on which this chapter is based, we were aiming to create as systematic and comprehensive a picture as possible of the cultural uses to which YouTube was being put, working within the constraints and architecture of the platform, and with the tools and methods that were available to us at the time. We wanted to step back from moral panics about young people, debates about the destruction of the existing media business, copyright infringement, or the triviality of cat videos, and get a broader sense of what kinds of content people were actually creating, sharing, and engaging with, on an average day, week, or month on the platform. Here, the exercise shared some continuity of approach with early studies of television that, as Ramon Lobato (2017) has outlined, looked at TV schedules 'to measure trends in TV programming, in terms of the prevalence of certain program types, genres, production sources/contexts, or specific textual attributes' (Lobato, 2017: 3); an approach that Lobato has proposed we might extend for the study of Netflix's constantly changing and internationally diverse catalogues (2017: 8–11).

Just as with schedule or catalogue studies of broadcast or streaming television, of course, studying patterns in the most popular content misses some of the material and social context in which YouTube's popular culture is made meaningful by audiences and content creators. YouTube videos circulate and are made sense of on the web, on mobile devices, and on television screens; they are embedded in posts across the web and social media; discussed and co-watched in living rooms, workplaces, bars, buses, and trains; and they are produced in specific everyday and/or professional settings, within networks of creators and organisations. But our content-centred viewpoint, and the deep immersion in the platform's culture that the coding exercise itself required, did allow us to identify a number of highly distinctive formal patterns and sociocultural trends associated with this still-emergent platform, which can then be read against these richer contexts.

The study drew on a sample of videos from four of YouTube's categories of popularity as they were in 2007 – Most Viewed, Most Favorited, Most Responded, and Most Discussed. Back then, these categories were plainly visible as tabs on the YouTube website,[1] and the platform provided simple ranked lists, inviting users to browse content based on what was popular across the entire global platform, rather than personalising or localising search results; and there was far less automated curation of content, so that the relationship between the user and what other users were watching was far more transparent than it is in the era of algorithmic content curation. Across these categories of popularity, 4,320 videos were gathered by sampling from six days across two weeks in each of three months of 2007 (August, October, and November). A coding system was developed by the research team over several months to categorise these videos according to textual and extra-textual features, coding for origin, uploader, genre, and themes. We did the coding manually, switching between a browser in which we watched hundreds of videos each, and the spreadsheets in which we were entering the data.

The coding scheme involved two top-level categories (with lower-level categories like form and genre considered in subsequent steps). These were, first, the apparent industrial *origin* of the video (whether it appeared to be user-created or the product of a traditional media company); and, second, the apparent identity of the *uploader* (whether a traditional media company, a small-to-medium enterprise or independent producer, a government organisation, cultural institution, or the like, or an amateur user). Our survey concentrated on the most popular videos within the period of the study (rather than looking at the most popular videos of all time), partly because it helped to order our sample, but also partly because we were trying to understand some of the more dynamic patterns in popular uses of YouTube.

However, in order to understand how popularity worked on YouTube, we need to do more than list, rank, and describe the most-watched videos. Returning to our discussion of popular culture in the opening chapter, is the 'popular' simply a matter of degree – measured by its reach or sales? Or is it a matter of kind – the cultural forms that are loved most intensely, or that are most 'of the people'? Even within early YouTube, content was represented as being more or less popular according to a range of different measures, including:

> *most viewed, most responded, most discussed, top rated, most favorited, previously popular,* and *most active*

We concentrated on four of these categories of popularity – Most Viewed, Most Favorited, Most Responded, Most Discussed – because we thought that comparing across them would give us a sense of the way different kinds of video content are made popular by audiences in different ways.

## How the Platform Has Shaped Popularity

The YouTube platform has not only reinforced the importance of popularity, it has also *shaped* popularity, through its design, its interface, and its rhetorical address to users. In 2007, when we completed data collection, the website users could see a visual representation of an apparently transparent 'database' – essentially just a series of ordered lists – of what was popular among the rest of the YouTube audience, and you could choose from among them (see Carrasco, 2013). The site has been progressively redesigned, alongside changing design conventions of the web and the shift to mobile apps, to direct us to content we might want to watch, including promoted content; logging in helps to deliver personalised content and to curate playlists. In 2017, navigation of the home page is reduced to endless scrolling and, once a user begins watching on most devices, the platform takes them on a potentially endless journey through 'related videos', selected and displayed via a proprietary algorithm.

While the system of curation and re-presentation to users was far less technologically sophisticated in 2007 than it is in 2017, even then the platform organised its content around metrics of popularity, each of which ordered YouTube according to a different logic of audience engagement. While all of these measures relied on quantitative assessments – that is, they all counted things – the categories Most Responded, Most Discussed, and Most Favorited provided a way to access platform-specific measures of attention that were different from those that had predominated audience measurement in the traditional broadcast media. Whereas Most Viewed most closely resembled the measures of attention used by the traditional media industries as a way of counting 'eyeballs in front of the screen', each of the other three measures provided some account of popularity based on activities that signalled a degree of participation in the YouTube community – if nothing else, all of them required the user to have an account and to be logged into the site. The Most Favorited category aggregated the videos popular enough to be added to a user's profile, and Most Discussed aggregated the videos that generated the most comments, whereas Most Responded recorded the videos that viewers were most frequently prompted to post a video response to, either by filming their own material or linking to another video on the platform. This 'video response' feature was removed from the platform in 2013.

Because it compared types of content across these measures of popularity, this content survey tells us more than just what was 'on' YouTube at this point in its early history. And because we were looking at a sample of the most *popular* videos, the results of this content survey are not simply a reflection of the collective tastes of the YouTube audience at the time. Each of these ways of measuring popularity also generated a different emphasis, and hence suggested a different interpretation of what YouTube was, and how it was being used. Of course, in some ways, the metrics did just what we might think – they measured the relative popularity of individual videos over a given time period, according to various criteria. But this is not all they did, and it is not all that social media metrics do now. They are not representations of reality, but technologies of re-presentation. Because they communicate to the audience what counts as popular on YouTube, these metrics also take an active role in creating the reality of what is popular on YouTube: metrics are not only descriptive or representational; they are also performative.

Michel Callon (1998) makes the argument that economic theories of markets 'format' real markets by making them calculable, and therefore affecting the choices of real actors who participate in those markets. This is not the same as saying that the 'discourses' of markets 'socially construct' our choices; rather, our models and understandings of markets function technologically, producing knowledge that can be used in practice, but only within the constraints of the ways this knowledge is structured and presented. The various measures of popularity within early YouTube functioned similarly: to a certain extent they made calculable and measurable a simplified and atomised model of audience engagement – based on the raw frequencies of views, comments, response videos, and additions to users' favourites. In turn, such metrics shape the character of the most popular content – users can either deliberately attempt to produce content that will generate large-scale attention according to the preset criteria, metrics, and algorithms, or they can ignore them altogether (and receive attention from dramatically smaller audiences). As with the mainstream media interpretations of what YouTube is for, this produces a feedback loop between the perceived uses of and value logics of YouTube; and its 'actual' uses and meanings.

The metrics we were using for this study simply no longer exist as part of the platform's user interface. The platform's significant and continuous design changes have worked not only to 'modernise' the look and feel of the website, but also to change the way the user is positioned in relation to YouTube's affordances. There have been fundamental architectural changes to the way popularity is both constructed and shaped via the much more personalised and social algorithms for search and front page layout, algorithmic search, and features like autoplaying 'related videos', which also relies on a propri-etary algorithm (Rieder et al., 2017). But, as various authors have pointed out, these algorithmic functions emerge out of the interactions among a number of stakeholders, actors, and interests – they may automate but they do not work autono-mously of human input and intent (Gillespie, 2016), leading Rieder et al (2017) to use the term 'ranking cultures' to incor-porate algorithms and the cultural contexts that design and are shaped by them. Postigo (2016) further notes how metrics shape the choices and performances of YouTubers, thereby intensifying the winner-take-all economics and driving the culture of the platform in directions that also serve the com-pany's interests, turning participation into 'YouTube money'.

Metrics are also part of YouTube's business ecology. A number of ancillary services, intermediaries, and start-ups have been built on YouTube audience and attention met-rics and data analytics. For example, launched in 2010 by YouTube itself, the YouTube Trends blog trades in data-driven observations, data visualisations, and analyses of cultural trends in YouTube, at the same time surfacing and highlighting particular aspects of YouTube's popular culture. Socialblade is among the most prominent of these ancillary platforms, providing close to real-time updates on popular-ity on YouTube, focusing on channels rather than videos. In order to demonstrate their value to creators, many MCNs incorporate metrics or partner with metrics services. Many of these services are connected into the commercial creator and advertising ecology, playing an active as well as represen-tational and performative role in constructing the shape and character of popularity on YouTube.

## The Two YouTubes: Traditional and User-Created Content

As we discussed in the previous chapter, during the first five years of YouTube's existence, the ways it was understood and discussed often relied on a binary division between 'professional' and 'amateur' content and uses. On the one hand, YouTube was an emerging or potential platform for the distribution of professional content – content drawing on recognisable media forms and genres, produced by paid professionals inside the formal media or music industries. On the other hand, it was an open platform for the creation and sharing of amateur content – drawing on vernacular forms and genres, produced by unpaid, non-professional individuals operating outside these industries. As is evident in these definitions, the categories of 'professional' and 'amateur' content usually conflate the dimensions of political economy, producer identity, and form or genre. In our study, we separated out these dimensions, resulting in a number of new categories that, when combined, allowed us to develop an understanding of how new configurations of these dimensions were emerging and forming distinctive genres, practices, and creative identities as the platform changed over time. As discussed in the 'Accounting for Popularity' section above, we separated out these dimensions as: 'origin'; 'uploader'; 'genre'; and 'themes'.

Given the concerns in 2007 around the extent that YouTube was indiscriminately allowing users to upload pirated content from traditional media and that this infringing use may have been its primary purpose, our first task was to attempt to assess the 'origin' dimension. We wanted to know what proportions of the most popular content appeared to have come from traditional media sources such as television, the cinema, or the music industry, which we labelled 'traditional media'; and what proportion appeared to have been created outside of those industries – and we labelled this category 'user-created content'.

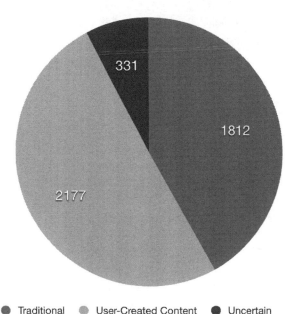

● Traditional    ● User-Created Content    ● Uncertain

Figure 3.1. Content Type Overall

The dichotomy between 'user-created' and 'traditional' media content is of course ever more problematic for understanding YouTube as a site of new convergences of or intermediate positions between these two categories. Nevertheless, in 2007 it still made some sense, and this division provided a useful organising framework for our large-scale content survey.

True to the 'Broadcast Yourself' promise of YouTube, the survey of the most popular content was weighted, just slightly, in favour of user-created videos. Just over half the material, or 2,177 videos, were coded as coming from user-created sources – content produced outside of the mainstream, broadcast, or established media. A majority (nearly 40%) of these videos were vlogs, the conversational form that had already become emblematic of YouTube's vernacular genres. Other genres included user-created music videos (15%) – including fanvids

and anime music videos; live material (13%) – musical performances, sporting footage, and 'slice of life' footage; and
informational content (10%) such as newscasts, video-game
reviews, and interviews. Scripted material (8%) such as sketch
comedy, animation, and machinima – animation made using
video-game engines often created by capturing and editing
choreographed gameplay – all made up a small part of the
sample. New or unclassifiable genres, many of them exhibiting a fascination with the manipulation of technique rather
than following any established form (discussed below), made
up around 10 per cent of the sample.

But there was a surprisingly small number of amateur,
mundane, 'slice of life' videos in the sample of most popular
videos – despite the myth, we just didn't come across very
many cat videos at all. Nor were there *any* videos of children
brutalising each other, 'happy slapping' innocent victims, or
'hooning' around the neighbourhood. This is not to deny the
presence of this material in early YouTube (clearly, it was
there somewhere, along with knitting videos and vintage documentaries), but it did not appear in this sample of YouTube's
most popular content.

Almost 42 per cent of the sample (1,812 videos) appeared
to come from traditional media sources – videos originally
produced within the established media industry, and frequently taken from an original source such as a television
broadcast or a DVD, and then uploaded to the website without a substantial amount of editing. Popular genres here
included informational programing (30%), which collected
clips from major news services in the US, the UK, and Latin
America, particularly material featuring 2008 US presidential candidates, celebrity interviews, and appearances on talk
shows, as well as portions from reality television programing.
Scripted materials (21%) made up the next-largest category,
and included sketch comedy, animation, and segments from
soap operas from Turkey and the Philippines. Videos from
traditional media sources also included live content (17%) –

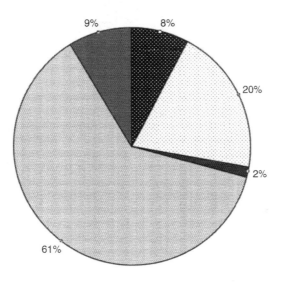

9%    8%

20%

2%

61%

■Traditional  □SME/Indie  ■Organization  ▨User  ■Uncertain

Figure 3.2.  Uploader Types

predominantly sports footage, clips from US primary debates, and music videos (13%), which came mostly from US Top40 artists. The final significant category included promotional materials (11%) – trailers for films and advertisements for products. Based on their titles and other studies of copyright content on YouTube,[2] it is probably the case that most of the videos that could not be coded because they had been removed came from traditional media sources.

Most of the videos seemed to have been uploaded by people outside established, mainstream media companies (see Figure 3.2). This group – coded as 'users' – was responsible for contributing a majority of the content in the sample – around 60 per cent. Traditional media companies and large rights holders, a group that includes television networks such as NBC and organisations such as the NBA (National Basketball Association), who have traditionally patrolled their

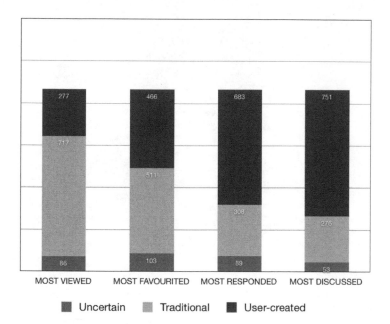

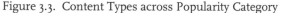

Figure 3.3. Content Types across Popularity Category

intellectual property rights fiercely on YouTube, made up only a fraction of the uploaders – about 8 per cent. Between these two categories was a group described as 'Small-to-medium enterprises (SMEs) or Independent producers (indies)', those working within the professional media industry but outside the domains of big-media organisations. This group accounted for nearly 20 per cent of the content uploaded.

When we compare user-created and traditional media across measures of popularity, some striking differences in how popular content was used began to emerge (see Figure 3.3).

While user-created content dominated the sample over-all, and 'users' appeared to comprise the largest group of people contributing to the system, not all of the categories of popularity were dominated by user-created content. Though traditional media and large rights holders made up a small percentage of the overall uploaders – not surprising, given the generally suspicious and cautious attitude taken by the majority of traditional media players we discussed in the previous chapter – content from broadcast and mass media sources comprised a significant proportion of the videos coded in the Most Viewed and Most Favorited (see Figure 3.3). Indeed, material from broadcast and mass media sources made up two-thirds of the Most Viewed category, where the largest genres were informational material – particularly news footage, political discussion, celebrity gossip, and interviews; live content – especially sports footage and live musical acts; and scripted programing – clips from television series, soap operas, and dramas, as well as animation and some sketch comedy. This content came mostly from television, but was mostly uploaded by users rather than by the traditional media and large rights holders themselves. User-created content in the Most Viewed category predominantly took the form of vlog entries, though there was also some instructional content, user-created sketch comedy, and musical performances – either footage from shows or users at home (or in the studio) performing directly for the camera.

The Most Favorited category – videos users had added to their personal profiles – was almost evenly split between traditional (47%) and user-created content (43%). 'Favoriting' something was an act both of self-expression and identity performance; when videos were added to a user's list of favourites, they were not just saved for later viewing; they were published as markers of personal taste and implicitly communicate recommendations to other users. As at September 2017, this feature is no longer available on the platform – instead, it is possible to 'share' (via a large number of other social media platforms), save for later, or add to a playlist.

A portion of videos in each category of popularity was coded as 'uncertain'; these videos, comprising roughly 10 per cent in the case of both Most Favorited and Most Viewed, included videos the coders were unable to make a definitive decision about. Many of the videos coded here had been removed from YouTube, and were undiscoverable on other video-sharing sites or elsewhere across the Internet. Others were from media systems coders were not familiar with – perhaps in a language other than English, Spanish, or Chinese – and coders were unable to read the formal, aesthetic, and extra-textual markers to determine the video's origin. Finally, some videos were coded as 'uncertain' in instances where coders could not clearly determine whether the content was user-created or the product of professional media producers, based on the content of the video and details provided in any intertextual or extra-textual sources, such as the profile of the uploader, hypertext links that might be provided to other sites on the Internet, or discussion in industry, press, or other publications regarding the videos.

These 'uncertain' videos reveal some of the most interesting difficulties that arise when classifying the content of YouTube. In practice, there was already a great deal of slippage between the categories of 'traditional media' and 'user-created content' in our survey, and making determinations between them relies as much on how the material is positioned by extra-textual and intertextual material as it does on markers within the content itself. But these problems were also very productive for our overall project: the coding process revealed some of the specific sources of uncertainty around the distinctions between professional and user-created content in YouTube.

## Clips and Quotes: Uses of Traditional Media Content

Like all media, YouTube only really makes sense when understood in the context of everyday life, and this is true of the patterns we observed in how audiences were making use of 'traditional media content'. In his (2008) book on 'produsage', Axel Bruns noted that open and participatory web and digital media tools (like blogging platforms, for example) meant audiences no longer needed to resort to auxiliary media forms to respond to the culture around them, suggesting the everyday experience of media audiencehood might need to be rethought to include new forms of cultural production that occur as part of ordinary media use. Participants in early YouTube clearly did engage in new forms of 'publishing', partly as a way to narrate and communicate their own cultural experiences, including their experiences as 'citizen-consumers', which are bound up with commercial popular media. Observing changes in the media and information environment in the mid 2000s, John Hartley (2008a) described this mode of cultural meaning making as 'redaction' – 'the production of new material by the process of editing existing content'. For Hartley, redaction is:

> a form of production not reduction of text (which is why the more familiar term 'editing' is not quite adequate). Indeed, the current moment could be characterised as a redactional society, indicating a time when there is too much instantly available information for anyone to see the world whole, resulting in a society that is characterised by its editorial practices. (Hartley, 2008a: 112)

Hartley (2008a: 19–35) argues that, in digital culture, the origin of meaning has migrated along the 'value chain' of the cultural industries, from the 'author', the 'producer', and the text, to the 'citizen-consumer', so that 'consumption' is a source of value creation, and not only its destination. Media consumption, under such a model, has moved away from being a 'read-only' activity to becoming a 'read–write' one.

This concept of redaction provides an alternative to the discourses of copyright infringement that dog the debates and corporate negotiations around the posting of traditional media content to YouTube. While some of the videos coded 'uncertain' discussed above had either been made private or removed by users, the majority were flagged as being unavailable as a result of copyright infringement claims. A small portion was also unavailable apparently due to Terms of

Use violations. This could signal a violation of YouTube's (at the time, very loosely defined) policies around offensive content, or it may have been the result of the user uploading copyrighted content – also a violation of the YouTube Terms of Use. So the amount of popular material originally from traditional media sources was probably larger than our results suggest, given that the videos were removed during the period between capturing and coding the data.[3]

There were several instances in this sample where the type of uploads media companies such as Viacom seemed to dread most appeared – entire episodes of programing divided into sections. In particular, the sample included two soap opera series, one each from the Philippines and Turkey. Not only was this material flagged as copyright-infringing fairly quickly but, in both instances, the videos made for a poor-quality viewing experience. Although in early 2008 YouTube had begun to make announcements about the introduction of high-definition video,[4] up until this point the low quality of YouTube videos and the ten-minute time limit imposed on uploads had made it an inferior method for 'illegally' distributing proprietary content, especially compared with protocols such as BitTorrent, and compression technologies such as DivX and Xvid supported by some other video-sharing services. As early as March 2006 YouTube had already begun enforcing a ten-minute limit on video uploads, precisely for these reasons, as they explained in a blog entry accompanying the change:

> If most of our users are uploading and watching short form video clips, why even bother to make the change? If it ain't broke, don't fix it right? Well, if you've followed our blog postings or any of the press articles, you know we're constantly trying to balance the rights of copyright owners with the rights of our users. We poked around the system a bit and found that these longer videos were more likely to be copyrighted videos from TV shows and movies than the shorter videos posted. ('Your 15 Minutes of Fame', 2006)

But a closer look at examples from our study shows that the uploading of short clips of traditional media content to the website was part of a more sophisticated range of cultural practices than simply the attempt to 'fileshare' or to avoid nationally or commercially bound distribution systems. Early YouTube contained a wealth of short video 'quotes'[5] – snippets of material users shared to draw attention to the most significant portion of a program. In terms of cultural analysis, the practice of quoting is quite distinct from that of uploading entire programs. Understanding YouTube as a redactional system, uploading proprietary content is at least partly a meaning-making process, rather than only an attempt to evade the constraints of mainstream media distribution mechanisms. Particularly through this practice of uploading media 'quotes', YouTube has functioned as a central clearing house service that people use as a way to catch up on public media events, as well as to break new stories and raise awareness of events – and in 2017 YouTube remains a significant repository of eyewitness footage as well as an archive of TV news reports.

When video of campus police using a Taser on UCLA student Mostafa Tabatabainejad was posted to YouTube in November of 2006, the citizen journalism potential of YouTube was elevated to the attention of the US national press. Frequently, however, quoted materials in the Most Viewed category tended to reflect the topics already at the top of public news agendas rather than breaking new stories. So we saw, for instance, quite a number of highlights packages from qualifying matches for the 2008 UEFA European Football Championship, which started in August 2007.

Unsurprisingly, given the US-dominated nature of the platform, the 2008 US presidential election campaign was well represented in the sample, in the form of campaign materials, debates, and press clips, as well as commentary, discussion, and debate. This was to be expected, given the increasingly significant role YouTube had already played as a site for both top-down and grass-roots political campaigning in the US (Shah and Marchionini, 2007). The presence of such material could be taken as an indication of a significant degree of engagement in US politics by the YouTube community, and on popular rather than official terms. But arguably, the forms of political engagement hinted at in these videos had just as much to do with celebrity culture (Couldry and Markham, 2007) as they had to do with deliberative processes or formal political culture – in the same way as the tabloid mainstream media tends to focus on individual candidates as media personalities. Highlighting the effects on political life of the heightened and personalised media attention John Thompson (2005) called the 'new visibility', politicians' stances on issues and their positions on the political spectrum in some ways are nothing but backstory for the front-stage drama of their media appearances and 'gotcha' moments. In the case of the minor Republican US presidential candidate Ron Paul, the YouTube activity around the election represented a concerted and organised attempt to (perhaps mischievously) drive up the popularity of an underdog candidate in defiance of the priorities set up by the mainstream media and the Democratic and Republican parties themselves. This pattern was a relatively benign, early harbinger of the rise of populism, the power of troll armies, and the centrality of social media platforms in contemporary electoral and national politics – developments that by the end of 2017 had become of significant and widespread public concern. In 2017, platforms like Facebook, Twitter, and YouTube were only just beginning to be held to account for their role in supporting or undermining the communicative processes necessary to democracy (Gillespie, 2017).

In the light of our earlier discussions about the importance of understanding YouTube as part of everyday media use, it is especially significant that music videos were prominent in the Most Favorited category. Music was central to the formation of other social networking services and social media platforms like MySpace (boyd, 2007), where it played a significant role as a marker of identity in user profiles, particularly of teens. The appearance of music videos as a significant content type of Most Favorited videos in early YouTube was a sign of things to come: whether in the form of Top-40 official music videos or bedroom guitar covers, as at 2017 music remains one of YouTube's strongest 'verticals', and YouTube dominates online music streaming overall – making up 46% of all online music streaming time according to an industry report (McIntyre, 2017).

The patterns of cultural tastes and practices observed in our study are undoubtedly related to those associated with the dominant forms of contemporary US popular culture more broadly – characterised by an engagement with dominant media events like the 2008 US presidential election; and by a preference for humour, vernacular video, Top-40 music and teen idols, tabloid culture, and celebrity gossip. But there was already a certain 'YouTube-ness' to these patterns as well. The intensity of engagement around *particular* bands, artists, celebrities, and video genres was at least partly produced within YouTube itself – how else to explain the fact that Ron Paul was, at times, more important to YouTube's attention economy than either Barack Obama or Hillary Clinton; or the Jonas Brothers more adored than any other pop artist? The patterns that emerged from the content survey hint at the shape of YouTube's common culture – a 'structure of feeling' neither unique to YouTube nor mirroring traditional popular and media culture, but instead a platform-specific hybrid of the two.

## Vaudeville to Vlogs: User-Created Content

User-created content made up more than two-thirds of the content coded in both the Most Responded and Most Discussed categories, where it comprised 63 and 69 per cent respectively – a dramatically higher percentage than traditional media content, especially when compared to the Most Viewed category, where the situation was reversed, with around two-thirds of the videos coded as traditional media content. As noted above, the sample included some but not large numbers of many of the prototypical user-created video forms. There were a few mundane videos, short films, fanvids, and mashups, as well as anime music videos, instructional video-game walk-throughs, and examples of machinima (short narrative films composed from edited gameplay footage).

Whatever the specific form, there were several observable aesthetic trends across the range of user-created content, indicative of the kinds of practices and values associated with an emerging medium. Frequently, the aesthetics of these user-created videos were especially concerned with experimentation with the video form, an explicit foregrounding of the medium itself that has historically been associated with the emergence of new media technologies, which Jenkins (2006c) suggests resembles the technological and aesthetic experimentation of early vaudeville.

In many of the most popular user-created videos there was a noticeable focus on video as a technology, and on the showcasing of technique rather than of artistry – an aesthetic pattern we saw continuing as users experimented with the radical constraints and looping function of the Vine platform, which limited videos to 6 seconds in length, or with the related artform of the animated GIF (Miltner and Highfield, 2017). Similarly, in the early years of YouTube, trick videos were popular with the YouTube community – using green-screen technology, split screens, or reversed footage, as well as the use of techniques to foreground the technology itself, for example the use of sound processing to produce 'silly' comic voices. Two good examples of the creative combination of a trick concept with the capabilities of video recording and editing techniques are 'What Song is This?' in which the Star Spangled Banner is sung backwards live, and then the footage is reversed to reveal the song;[6] and 'The Original

Human TETRIS Performance by Guillaume Reymond',[7] a stop-motion animation in which a group of people dressed in various colours arrange and rearrange themselves in formation to imitate the progress of a game of Tetris, accompanied by an accurate *a cappella* version of the Tetris soundtrack. Indeed, both of these videos were nominees for the 'Creative' category in the 2007 YouTube awards, a short-lived initiative which continued only until 2008 (later replaced by the Streamy Awards, co-produced by ancillary publication *Tubefilter* and focusing more on vlog-style YouTube acts).[8]

Another good illustration of this early experimental fascination with the technological capabilities of digital video editing is the category of videos referred to by their producers as 'YouTube Poop'. Emerging as a faddish genre of their own, these often-frenetic videos pieced together found television footage into irreverent, often nonsensical, works. They showed a particular fascination with Saturday morning cartoons from the 1990s (particularly 'low' American cartoons such as *The Super Mario Bros. Super Show!*) and television commercials, though there were also 'poops' made for anime series and videos from YouTube itself.[9] The edits are often abrupt and jarring, and the audio is manipulated through quick cuts, changing speeds, and the introduction of alternative soundtracks. The result frequently foregoes narrative and resembles something most akin to parody or video art. Throughout the user-created content in our survey, regardless of the techniques used, the sample points clearly to a logic of cultural value centred for the most part around novelty and humour; as well as the apparently endless generativity of the remix.

But it was vlog (videoblog) entries that dominated the sample, making up nearly 40 per cent of the videos coded at Most Discussed and just over a quarter of the videos coded at Most Responded. The prevalence of vlog entries is significant, given it is an almost exclusively user-created form of online video production. Vlogging itself is not necessarily new or unique to YouTube, but it is an emblematic form of YouTube participation. The form has antecedents in webcam culture, personal blogging, and the more widespread 'confessional culture' (Matthews, 2007) that characterises television talk-shows and reality television focused on the observation of everyday life; but there was also a relatively small but intensely engaged community of videobloggers on the web for several years before YouTube. As Trine Bjørkman Berry argues, 'many of the commonplace practices we see on YouTube, Vine, Snapchat and other video sites were developed for a digital environment by the early community of videobloggers' (2015: 195), publishing Quicktime videos on custom platforms before the breakthrough innovation in backend transcoding, publishing, and streaming that YouTube afforded.

The success of Ze Frank (real name Hosea Jan Frank) was important in publicly defining a particular version of the genre and establishing its possibility as a bona fide mode of cultural production, despite the fact it did not appear on YouTube. His twelve-month vlogging project, 'the show with ze frank', which ran from 16 March 2006 to 16 March 2007, established some of the formal characteristics of the genre in the form it has been remediated and taken up in YouTube, particularly in terms of the reliance on comedy, rapid editing and snappy performance to camera.

The simple format of the videoblog also lends itself to a range of forms and formats, often drawing on live perfor- mance traditions – and in its variety, it is similar to the vaudeville tradition of the late nineteenth and early twentieth centuries. Henry Jenkins (2006c; see also Butsch, 2000) notes that vaudeville functioned as a relatively open platform for a wide range of short acts, each of which was kept under twenty minutes; and without directors, actors chose their own material and refined their skills based on direct audience feedback. There was a reliance on emotion in order to create the memorable and the spectacular. Vlogging shares this emphasis on liveness, immediacy, and conversation. These characteristics of YouTube's most prominent genre are essential for understanding the particularity of YouTube, as well as being fundamental to contemporary media entertainment engagement across social media platforms.

The vlog emphasises the persistent cultural importance of interpersonal face-to-face communication and continues to provide an important point of difference between online video and television. Not only is the vlog relatively easy to produce in technical terms, generally requiring little more than a webcam, a good sense of timing, and basic editing skills, it is a form whose persistent direct address to the viewer inherently invites feedback. While television content – news, sketch comedy, clips from soap operas – may draw people to the service for a catch-up, traditional media content doesn't explicitly invite conversational and inter-creative (Spurgeon, 2008; Meikle, 2002) participation, as might be measured by the numbers of comments and video responses. It seems that, more than any other form in the sample, the vlog as a genre of communication invites critique, debate, and discussion. Direct response, through comment and via video, is central to this mode of engagement. Early vlogs were frequently responses to other vlogs, carrying out discussion across YouTube and directly addressing comments left on previous vlog entries. Patricia Lange (2007a) noted that particularly engaged first-generation YouTubers directly addressed negative comments and 'hating' through their vlogs, many seeing this as an inherent part of the form and culture of vlogging – and these practices are firmly embedded in the professional conventions of the most successful YouTubers. Early in her career as an amateur YouTube comedian, for example, popular YouTuber Natalie Tran (communitychannel) devoted part of each video to displaying and responding to comments that had been left on her previous video, folding this audience engagement into the ongoing comedy routine itself; as at October 2017 she had close to 1.9 million subscribers.

Two other significant genres that were both Most Discussed

and Most Responded were informational content and music videos. The former included user-created newscasts, interviews, documentaries, and a number of videos that would bleed over into the vlog category – they frequently critiqued popular media or comment on 'YouTube dramas' through visual juxtaposition, or by adding commentary or on-screen graphics. Many user-created music videos also adopted a vlog-style conversational mode, as artists preface their work with a discussion of the motivations or context for the piece they have written or will perform, and respond to suggestions and feedback, often drawing the audience into the intimacy afforded by direct address. It was this conversational character that distinguished the mode of engagement in the categories dominated by user-created content from those dominated by traditional media. Indeed, the vaudevillian vlog is arguably the ur-genre of commercial 'social media entertainment' (Cunningham and Craig, 2017) – but it was developed, elaborated, and refined in early YouTube's vernacular culture.

## Identifying Uploaders: Beyond the Professional and Amateur Divide

Our 2007 content survey showed that YouTube's popular videos were already being contributed by a range of professional, semi-professional, amateur, and pro-amateur participants, some of whom produced content that was an uncomfortable fit with the available categories of either 'traditional' media content or the vernacular forms generally associated with the concept of 'amateur' content. University lectures and educational materials, such as those uploaded by early adopter institutions including the University of New South Wales[10] and the University of California, Berkeley,[11] online presentations developed by Google for forthcoming products like the Android mobile operating system, or even footage of military aircraft landing, somewhat inexplicably uploaded by the Royal Australian Air Force's official channel[12]

– each of these was an early example of content that strained to fit anywhere in relation to the traditional media/user-created content dichotomy. While these were early adopters, from the 2010s onward YouTube was increasingly one of several mainstream social media platforms on which universities, businesses, and government departments generally could be expected to have a presence.

We also uncovered early examples of creative businesses using YouTube as a platform for audience engagement. Ford Models, for example, were using YouTube both for promotional purposes and to identify talent.[13] Ford was not a traditional media company; despite their relatively large size as a business, their success on YouTube was a result of them capitalising on the same self-publishing and conversational opportunities as individual videobloggers and bedroom musicians. The material Ford was producing – make-up tips, model profiles, fashion guidelines, and modelling tutorials – could conceivably be packaged for broadcast as fashion programing on cable or broadcast television. But outside of the broadcast flow and contextualised within a branded YouTube channel, these videos appeared and were consumed as organic YouTube content; it is only the professional quality of the content and the corporate size of the uploader that would mark Ford Models as a professional outfit – the platform itself at that time was almost completely agnostic to the issue of professional status. Since then, of course, the beauty-centred lifestyle influencer industry has grown dramatically, and beauty or fashion vlogs (featuring infomercial-style content like make-up and hair tips, wrapped in an intimate form of address) are as firmly embedded in the social media marketing industry as make-up ads were in broadcast television (Nazerali, 2017; Berryman and Kavka, 2017).

Similarly, even in 2008 the category of 'user' was complicated by made-for-web video start-ups, such as JumpTV Sports, who put together sports packages and delivered content to a range of sports sites around the world, and

NoGoodTV, who produced risqué, masculine, programing. Many of these uploaders resemble traditional television producers using the Internet as a way to distribute niche programing or specialised content without needing to negotiate cable or television distribution deals. NoGoodTV's content, for instance, resembled the laddish programing regularly seen on cable channels in the US such as Spike (a Viacom brand) and the video-game oriented G4 TV. It was a mixture of music videos, celebrity interviews, sketches, informational programing, and miscellanea, wrapped in on-screen graphics. Its resemblance to television content pointed to the way digital delivery options such as YouTube and the increasing move of material online were already destabilising medium-dependent definitions of media forms (Green, 2008); and were harbingers of media enterprises like RedBull TV, which has its own YouTube channel with 6.4m subscribers as at October 2017[14] as well as an extensive cross-platform presence and talent development arm.

So too, although videoblogging has always been a dominant form of user-created content and fundamental to YouTube's sense of community, not all vlogs are personal journal entries created in bedrooms. Indeed, a number of prominent vloggers were already quite clearly using YouTube as a business venture, and all of them still appeared to be going strong in 2017. Examples include comedian Nalts (Kevin Nalty, 238,000+ subscribers as at October 2017),[15] comedy/gaming vlogger Charlestrippy (836,000+),[16] and Australian 'tech geek' vlogger Blunty3000 (Nate Burr, 333,000+).[17] They were already participants in YouTube's Partner Program and drew revenue from their activities on YouTube. But unlike NoGoodTV, which seemed to import to YouTube a broadcast model or one-way model of audience engagement, these creators had always been active participants in the YouTube community. Even though creators like Charlestrippy used their vlogs and YouTube pages to advertise their expertise – in his case, creating viral videos – their online success was as much due to their grounded knowledge of and effective participation within YouTube's communicative ecology as it was the savvy with which they produced content, and they were virtuosic in their mastery of YouTube's home-grown forms and practices.

In 2007–8, some artists represented by large labels had already taken up this mode as a way to engage and manage their fan communities. English/Portuguese singer-songwriter Mia Rose is a good example of this.[18] Rose represented herself as an independent artist, using YouTube to sell her content by reaching out across the social network to connect with her audiences. Her position as something other than 'commercial artist' or 'amateur musician' was highlighted by the fact that, in our study, she was identified as both a 'user' and an independent producer by different coders. In April 2008, after the sample had been captured, she signed to the combined music, fashion, and lifestyle company NextSelection Lifestyle Group and became a managed artist. Her channel remained unchanged in the following year, however, still projecting the same home-grown brand image with which it began. As at October 2017 it had 340,700 subscribers and had evolved into a fairly generic, professionally produced lifestyle channel, with cooking, shopping, and beauty vlogs (clearly featuring brand endorsements) interspersed with regular song releases, and folksy 'bedroom' acoustic musical performances.

Beyond such apparently accidental or viral success in crossing the amateur–professional boundary, in the six years since this study was first conducted we have seen significant and deliberate strategies on behalf of YouTube, Inc., to bring the two together. For example, in 2011 YouTube acquired viral video production company and proto-MCN Next New Networks (Diana, 2011; Miller, 2011). Also in 2011, YouTube produced and promoted the 'YouTube Creator Playbook', an instructional resource designed to help creators optimise their content and audience engagement strategies on YouTube, which explicitly highlighted the value of the social media and community-centred approaches developed and refined by early YouTube videobloggers.[19] In 2011 YouTube also started the NextUp Program (which was still running in 2016) to identify, incentivise, and develop potential 'star' content creators in a range of key genres;[20] beginning in London in 2012, the company has progressively established bricks-and-mortar YouTube Spaces – talent incubator studios for aspiring YouTubers – in media-intensive cities around the world.[21] As at October 2017, there were YouTube Spaces in Berlin, London, Los Angeles, Mumbai, New York, Paris, Rio, São Paulo, Tokyo, and Toronto – with YouTube creator events, roadshows, and camps taking place at various other locations over the years, offering opportunities for YouTubers at various levels of professionalisation to become increasingly sophisticated media producers, performers, and brand managers.

Meanwhile, YouTube's deep reserves of apparently chaotic vernacular creativity and the genres that emerge from it are also an essential differentiating part of YouTube's brand, as is constantly reinforced by YouTube's own public representations of its culture, particularly when addressing the user community. For example, on its seventh birthday in 2012, the video that YouTube released in an act of celebration and self-memorialisation, just as television has always been wont to do (see Hartley et al., 2007), heavily emphasised amateur content creators and vernacular video forms.[22] Celebrating their tenth birthday in 2015 – the same year they launched the premium subscription app YouTube Red – YouTube posted a video called 'The A-Z of YouTube', a dizzying montage of viral videos (from Keyboard Cat and Numa Numa to Gangnam Style) and key vernacular genres (beauty vloggers, It Gets Better, Kids React, and gameplay) set to an alphabet-themed rap (interrupted only by a brief Rickrolling reprise featuring audio of the infamous Rick Astley song 'Never Gonna Give You Up') and ending with 'thank you for your creativity, self-expression and fun'.[23]

The codes and conventions of vernacular online video underpinned YouTube's entrance into the original programing market in October 2011, when it announced the upcoming launch of original channels that featured people whom we might formerly have thought of as 'mainstream media' talent, but who had demonstrated social media savvy – Madonna, Jay Z, and Ashton Kutcher were among the names mentioned in the press release (Waxman, 2011). But ultimately, the original programing strategy for YouTube Red has consolidated around YouTube's most popular genres and home-grown stars, drawing on the content forms, genres, and practices pioneered by the first generation of YouTubers, in turn drawing on earlier vernacular cultures of the Internet, blogs and alternative media, and extending back to vaudeville and beyond.

On the one hand, YouTube and the new intermediaries surrounding the online video business are working to professionalise previously amateur YouTubers (Lobato, 2016; Cunningham and Craig, 2017). But, on the other hand, it is the vernacular aesthetics, techniques, and marketing practices originated and refined by early videobloggers that are consistently held up by YouTube as the gold standard for aspiring creators, and are at the heart of the YouTube brand. From early YouTube through to 2017, while the culture of YouTube has evolved and its interests in the media business have expanded, it has retained certain cultural logics, genres, and practices that are part of its DNA – distinctive cultural features that we might call YouTube's 'platform vernaculars' (Gibbs et al., 2015).

## From Videos and Views to Channels and Subscribers

While most of this chapter has focused on YouTube's popular culture at the level of videos and genres, there is another, increasingly important, way of understanding popularity on YouTube, and that is at the level of the 'channel', and the number of subscribers each channel attracts. The 'most viewed videos' and 'most subscribed channels' sit at opposite ends of the spectrum of engagement on YouTube. The Most Viewed category for channels, as for videos, simply measures the number of times a particular channel page has been viewed – representing the channels that may not draw an especially high level of intensity or direct visible engagement, but have the greatest reach. The Most Subscribed category contains those channels that the most users want to follow (or, perhaps, publicly to be seen following). In aggregate it is a result of the actions of those users who have accounts on the platform, and it represents a collective performance of what the YouTube community values most; within the constraints of how the platform represents popularity and enables content discovery. Because it is thought to be a proxy for deep audience engagement and return visits, subscriber count is also the key metric of success and hence, for YouTubers, the key to unlocking revenue streams from sponsorship and merchandising, and the pathway to greater support from and leverage with the company.

As a 2016 *Tubefilter* article argued (Gutelle, 2016), while subscriber count is seen as a crude measure of audience engagement (and watch time, sharing, and commenting could be considered as well), 'the increasing number of million-subscriber channels is indicative of the exponential growth YouTube has experienced since its 2005 inception'. The article reported that, as at 23 February 2010 – YouTube's fifth birthday – 'there were only five channels with at least one million subscribers', a number that rose to 68 two years later, then to 594 two years after that, and another two years later, in 2016, there were 2,000 'YouTube millionaires' – and the views that went along with that were in the billions. *Tubefilter*'s regular YouTube Millionaires column regularly features these star YouTubers, interviewing them about the keys to their success – most often, reinforcing discourses of authenticity, community, and genuinely interactive audience or fan engagement.[24]

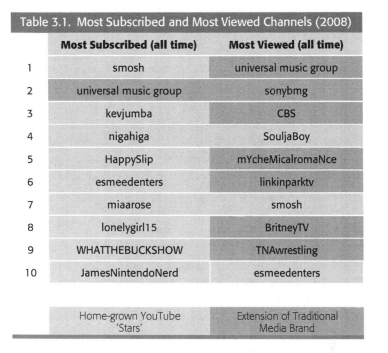

| | Most Subscribed (all time) | Most Viewed (all time) |
|---|---|---|
| 1 | smosh | universal music group |
| 2 | universal music group | sonybmg |
| 3 | kevjumba | CBS |
| 4 | nigahiga | SouljaBoy |
| 5 | HappySlip | mYcheMicalromaNce |
| 6 | esmeedenters | linkinparktv |
| 7 | miaarose | smosh |
| 8 | lonelygirl15 | BritneyTV |
| 9 | WHATTHEBUCKSHOW | TNAwrestling |
| 10 | JamesNintendoNerd | esmeedenters |
| | Home-grown YouTube 'Stars' | Extension of Traditional Media Brand |

Table 3.1. Most Subscribed and Most Viewed Channels (2008)

In YouTube's first five years, it was the first-generation YouTubers – and not the mainstream media players – who held the keys to audience engagement for which subscriber count is a proxy measure. The difference between the Most Subscribed (which required users to be signed up and signed in to the site) and the Most Viewed channels (a result of the viewing habits of all users, not just members) of all time as at February 2008 illustrated this clearly.

As Table 3.1 demonstrates, while traditional media companies were well represented in the Most Viewed list, the list of Most Subscribed channels was dominated by 'YouTube stars' – participants (whether strictly 'amateurs', SMEs, or even musicians backed by major labels) whose brands were developed within YouTube's social network. Their work covers a range of genres, from sketch comedy films (smosh) through celebrity news (WHATTHEBUCKSHOW), and comedy-style vlogging based around everyday life and personal identity (nigahiga, kevjumba, HappySlip). In comparison to the Most Viewed category, the list of Most Subscribed videos contains far fewer traditional media companies like music labels (such as Universal Music Group) or sports franchises (TNAwrestling), using YouTube as a platform for brand extension. Some of these (smosh, kevjumba, nigahiga, HappySlip) were among the most well-known and highly paid YouTubers in 2017. The genres they pioneered are mainstays of contemporary YouTube stars, as well as of the professional content developed by MCNs and YouTube themselves.

By 2013, it had become increasingly difficult to get at these statistics[25] – and casual users are certainly not invited to do so, instead being presented with algorithmically curated home pages with personalised video and channel suggestions based on personal viewing histories, other activity under the users' Google login; as well as those aggregated and highlighted by YouTube (under their official 'highlights' channel for each genre). However, the 'popular channels' list (worldwide, by number of subscribers) as at 22 May 2013[26] indicated a similar pattern, with YouTubers holding more than half the top spots, and popular music stars and aggregated official channels taking up the rest (see Table 3.2). The 'official' channels (called 'best of' in the YouTube browser or app) curate content under YouTube's key verticals; many of the videos included there represent key YouTube genres (videoblogs, game walkthroughs) but some, like 'News' and 'Music', curate content from 'official' media (like TV news) and music sources (the 'Music' channel pulls in official music videos from Vevo).

It is no longer possible, then, to view the most subscribed channels easily from within YouTube itself, because of the personalised logic of the site. But using the ancillary metrics service and MCN platform Socialblade, we can see the ten most-subscribed channels as at 23 October 2017 (see Table 3.3).[27]

The list of most subscribed channels in October 2017, if we extend down to thirty, contains home-grown YouTube chan-

| Table 3.2  Most Subscribed Channels (2013) |
| --- |
| **Most Subscribed** |
| smosh |
| RayWilliamJohnson |
| nigahiga |
| RihannaVEVO |
| PewDiePie |
| machinima |
| HolaSoyGerman |
| Movies [YouTube official] |
| OneDirectionVEVO |
| TV Shows [YouTube official] |

| Table 3.3  Most Subscribed Channels (2017) |
| --- |
| **Most Subscribed** |
| PewDiePie |
| YouTube Movies [YouTube official] |
| HolaSoyGerman |
| JustinBieberVEVO |
| T-Series |
| elrubiusOMG |
| Rihanna VEVO |
| YouTube Spotlight [YouTube official] |
| TaylorSwiftVEVO |
| KatyPerryVEVO |

nels across a range of genres (but particularly comedy, games, and sports; and mostly featuring young, male, talent), like Smosh, nigahiga, Fernanfloo, and Dude Perfect; but also a lot of big Top-40 music artists like Katy Perry, Eminem, Taylor Swift, OneDirection, and TheEllenShow.

Removing the 'official' curated channels from the list

Table 3.4  Top 10 Most Influential YouTubers by Socialblade Rank (2017)

| Username | Subscribers | Video Views |
| --- | --- | --- |
| T-series | 21.3 m | 20 bn |
| Ryan ToysReview | 8.3 m | 14 bn |
| LuisFonsiVEVO | 9 m | 4 bn |
| Canal KondZilla | 16 m | 7.7 bn |
| WorpointOfficial | 8.4 m | 6.3 bn |
| Jothair Em Pânico | 644,473 | 145 m |
| Netd müzik | 6 m | 14 bn |
| Ed Sheeran | 19 m | 8 bn |
| ABS-CBN Entertainment | 6 m | 8 bn |
| El Rieno Infantil | 7.6 m | 9.4 bn |

and viewing the Top 50 YouTubers worldwide based on Socialblade's 'SB rank' (a more engagement-focused metric which measures the relationships between subscribers counts (measured in the millions) – which can easily be gamed; views (in the billions) relative to the age and activity on the channel, and other undisclosed channel metrics), the top ten channels as at October 2017 are listed in Table 3.4.

Here we can see what really drives engagement on YouTube, from the perspective of the Socialblade Rank metrics – music, gameplay, and kids' content like unboxing videos and nursery rhymes (further down the list at twelfth place is LittleBabyBum, which specialises in nursery rhymes for young children). Indeed, for Australia and the UK, music and children's content dominate the top channels.

In the years since our original content analysis, while YouTube's in-house curation and content recommendation systems are driving subscriptions to official channels, in 2017 it was still true that the most subscribed channels (which is a measure of 'true' community in YouTube's own logics) tend to be those that are either built around star YouTubers, or 'mainstream' media properties that have a symbiotic relationship with the platform (as in the example of Katy Perry's live 'behind the scenes' stream; and as in the case of Ellen's regular crossover between vernacular YouTube content and her television show). The logics of a vernacular YouTube culture, and its platform-centric genres and forms – from gameplay to unboxing and videoblogging – remain essential to YouTube's identity and brand.

CHAPTER FOUR

# The YouTube Community

Participation in YouTube takes many different forms, from casual viewing, to binge-watching, to fandom, through to highly invested and intensive participation as a content creator – either as an amateur, a 'professionalising amateur' (Cunningham and Craig, 2017), a media company, or a brand. While all these different levels of participation are possible, very few users regularly upload videos, let alone actively maintain channels and audience engagement, on YouTube. But some YouTube content creators understand and discursively represent themselves as 'YouTubers', and as part of a YouTube *community*. For these users, YouTube works not only as a content delivery platform, but also as a social media platform. Unlike the more obviously 'social' platforms such as Facebook, where social connection is based on personal profiles and 'friending' (boyd and Ellison, 2007), in YouTube the video itself has long been a primary vehicle of social interaction and communication (Paolillo, 2008; Lange, 2007b), as well as peer learning, as we discuss below.

In this chapter, we focus on the early YouTube users who spent time on the platform contributing content, referring to, building on, and critiquing each other's videos, as well as collaborating (and arguing) with one another, as constituting the 'social core' (Paolillo, 2008) of this community; and in terms of innovation theory, a group of lead users who have collectively identified and exploited opportunities to improve the way YouTube worked through their own practices. We argue that the activities of these 'YouTubers' – a category that operates in the community itself as well as in academic discourse

(as in Lange, 2007a) – have always been very important driv-
ers of the attention economy of YouTube, and significant in
the co-creation of a particular version of YouTube's emergent
culture.

Community is a constitutive cultural logic of the platform,
bringing with it values and discourses around authenticity and
social connection to audiences, fans, and fellow YouTubers.
But this discourse of 'community' is also used strategically
by the platform, and like the term 'platform' itself (Gillespie,
2010) it may obscure as much as it reveals, and constrain as
much as it enables – and as we discuss in the final section
of this chapter, controversies in the contemporary YouTube
community help us to understand its limits.

## Platform as Patron

Platforms have specific affordances and user cultures, as
well as being companies with evolving business interests. As
companies, they have considerable influence on their cultures
of use; often enacted through changes in the sociotechnical
architectures and interfaces of the platform. YouTube has
taken an especially interesting journey from being tech-
focused and relatively agnostic about what content it supports,
to taking a much more active role in creator development
and in shaping the behavioural and cultural norms of the
platform. Just as wealthy nobles and rich industrialists have
been patrons of the arts for hundreds of years (thereby materially supporting and exerting control over, but not originating,
creative works), it is therefore useful to think of YouTube (the
company and the platform) as a modern-day patron of artists
(the YouTubers).

Following a similar line of argument, Virginia Nightingale
(2007) draws on the anthropologist Alfred Gell (1998)
to elaborate theories of agency and exchange in her study
of online photosharing and mobile media. As Nightingale
explains, Gell suggests that patronage partly predetermines

'the conditions under which the creative work is produced and the environment of reception in which the image is displayed' (Nightingale, 2007: 293). In the context of camera phones and image-sharing websites, 'industry players maintain the ongoing operational environment and offer "patronage" to site users'. Likewise, YouTube can be seen as the 'patron' of collective creativity, controlling and continuously reshaping some of the conditions under which creative content is produced, ordered, and re-presented for the interpretation of audiences. In previous chapters, we have described the ways in which, for example, the YouTube website's metrics of popularity order our understanding of what YouTube is for; as well as the impacts on early YouTube aesthetics of the platform's technical limits – many of which, such as the short video duration and the low resolution, no longer exist; and the shaping effect of the aesthetics and affordances of the user interface and content curation algorithms (Postigo, 2016).

But the purposes and meanings of YouTube as a cultural system have also been co-created by its users – albeit not in conditions of their making, and with very uneven levels of agency and control. Through their individual and collective activities – uploading, viewing, discussing, and collaborating – the YouTube community formed a complex, distributed network of creative practice and social interaction. Writing about the social worlds of various fields of cultural production, from modernist poetry to dancehall jazz and avant-garde music, Howard Becker (1982) described this kind of formation as an 'art world' – 'the network of people whose cooperative activity, organised via their joint knowledge of conventional means of doing things, produces the kind of art works that art world is noted for' (Becker, 1982: x). Becker's case studies demonstrate the ways that aesthetic principles and technologies are shared by producers, support workers, and audiences, and the way they organise, enable, and constrain the possible range of a particular artistic activity. The construction and negotiation of aesthetic values and 'proper' techniques, he argues, is not confined to academics or experts, but involves everyone who contributes to the process of cultural production, including audiences. Similarly, in YouTube, co-evolving aesthetic values, cultural forms, and creative techniques are normalised via the collective activities and judgements of the creator community (who enact the roles of both artists and audiences for each other's work) – forming an informal and emergent 'art world' specific to YouTube.

As patron, YouTube provides the supporting and constraining mechanisms of a system whose meaning is generated by the uses to which the website is put, and within which, collectively, users exercise agency. The political implications of this arrangement, however, are still contentious – with a steady stream of scholarship since the 1990s arguing that the participation of user communities can be read in terms of free labour (Terranova, 2000), or, as discussed earlier, a form of 'digital sharecropping' (Soha and McDowell, 2017). Critiques of the creative industries and, now, the 'sharing' or 'gig economy', point out the implications for the work conditions of aspiring creative practitioners and media professionals who are already under-compensated, and who work within conditions of 'precarious labour' (Deuze, 2007; Ross, 2000). Others are concerned with the various ways platform providers such as game publishers and social media companies profit directly from user productivity while simultaneously constraining users' rights (Humphreys, 2005) and, more recently, mining and exploiting their data (Andrejevic, 2013). The ever-intensifying datafication of ordinary social media activity and content sharing online has made it ever clearer that our activities are being monetised, raising the question of whether – even as audiences or consumers rather than creators – we are creating economic value for the big platforms, and whether or not the social contract implicit in these labour relations is just and fair. These labour debates have taken on a different cast with the rise of the aspirational, entrepreneurial social media influencer or YouTuber, particularly for feminist scholars, who focus on the affective and relational kinds of work involved (Duffy, 2017; Banet-Weiser, 2012).

Drawing largely on ethnographic work with both MMOG players and game developers in the mid 2000s, Banks and Humphreys (2008, n.p.) argued that these new relations of cultural production indicated a profound shift in which 'frameworks and categories of analysis (such as the traditional labour theory of value) that worked well in the context of an industrial media economy are perhaps less helpful than before'. They argued that these relationships in fact 'introduce a form of creative destruction to labour relations' in contexts where all the participants (including 'producers' as well as 'user co-creators') have mixed motivations, and where they work for a range of benefits. Some gamers engage in co-creative activities out of a passion for the game itself, others for the pleasures of achievement, others for social status within the game community, and still others in pursuit of commercial opportunities. As Banks and Humphreys also note, 'producers, programmers, artists, community development managers, and CEOs' have a wide range of often conflicting ideas about how the new collaborative and co-creative production processes of game environments should be managed, but that 'it is from these uneven, multiple and messy practices, motivations, negotiations, actants, and materials that participatory culture is being made and negotiated'.

Back in 2008, YouTube was a relatively new site of the same kinds of 'messy' and emergent relations among platform providers, content producers, and the audiences Banks and Humphreys described in the context of game culture. By 2017, YouTube was far more directly interventionist and overt in its role as patron of both commercial and non-commercial creator activity. YouTube enacts its role as patron through its Partner Program, through its Creator Spaces and meet-ups – where the company directly resources creative development and teaches marketing and audience engagement skills to its professionalising content creators. It also shapes content in certain directions through technical regulatory mechanisms that are not always transparent – such as 'demonetisation' and other means of making content less visible if it is seen to stray beyond the acceptable. In doing so, financial incentives like 'monetisation' are conflated with civic values and community norms on the platform, as the 2017 controversy around the 'adpocalypse' (discussed in further detail in the concluding chapter) demonstrates.

In the rest of this chapter, we investigate the way these new dynamics of creative work have played out in YouTube and how they are understood and negotiated in practice by the content creators who are primarily based on the platform – the 'YouTubers'. In the ordinary course of their cultural practice as YouTubers, these most visibly engaged users of YouTube actively participate in shaping, contesting, and negotiating the emergent culture of YouTube's social network, the idea of a YouTube community, and their relationships to the company's interests.

## YouTubers as Innovators

The YouTubers' community-building activities take place within an architecture that, while it embedded social networking features, was not primarily designed for collaborative or collective production. In comparison to other contemporary social networking sites built around user-created content, like Flickr and LiveJournal, and despite the rhetorical address to the YouTube 'community' in the company's official blog, the architecture of early YouTube did not overtly invite community-building, collaboration, or purposeful group work. Harley and Fitzpatrick (2008) note that the top-down conceit of YouTube as an alternative 'broadcaster' (rather than a social network) flowed through to interaction design elements that work to 'filter out' the social network aspects of the website for the casual or novice visitor or user; José van Dijck (2013) additionally argues that the site's focus has broadly shifted from 'homecasting' to broadcasting, repositioning users as consumers, rather than creators, by default. The website's visual design has always been dominated by thumbnails of videos, not user profiles, groups, or conversations. While the early iterations of the platform supported YouTube 'groups' for users to interact, they were far from easy to find using keyword searches and, like videos, they were ranked quantitatively.[2] The ban on downloading videos (based on copyright logics) and the limitations of user controls over open content licensing created serious barriers to collaborative production – there were no *overt* invitations to collaborate with other users, or to remix or quote each other's videos.

YouTube's interface design may not be elegant, but it is famously *usable*, at least within the limits of its assumed purpose – to upload, add metadata to, and publish videos; and at least for a majority of users. Indeed, its usability is undoubtedly one of the reasons for its mass popularisation. But this apparently seamless usability can also be seen another way – as both a constraint and an unstable compromise. Technologies designed for active user participation (like software, digital cameras, or YouTube itself) generally represent a compromise in design between two ideological extremes. As Burgess has written elsewhere in the context of smartphone design (Burgess, 2012b), at one end is the ideal of extreme *hackability* – 'where a given technology is perceived and presented as open-ended, manipulable, and affording complex experimentation with an accompanying level of difficulty' (Burgess, 2012b: 30). At the other is the ideal of extreme *usability* – 'where a technology is perceived and presented as allowing easy access to a pre-determined set of simple operations' (Burgess, 2012b: 30). Ideally, as technologies evolve, the tensions between these competing dynamics are never really resolved, opening up possibilities for highly usable and accessible technologies that are also expansible, adaptable, and malleable (Galloway et al., 2004), and so preserving the potential for the technologies to be 'generative' (Zittrain, 2008) of new or unexpected possibilities. Even the most usable and apparently simple technologies may offer creative possibilities that extend far beyond their most obvious, invited uses – possibilities most frequently realised or even pioneered by users, often to the surprise of the technology's designers.

Similarly, despite YouTube's design focus on usability and a simple and limited set of features, a number of interesting and innovative early uses of YouTube originated in the user community. For example, live video chat, which was already a popular activity elsewhere, had not been introduced as a YouTube service in 2007 because of perceived privacy risks (Stone, 2007). As a workaround, many of the most invested YouTubers were using relatively unregulated alternatives like Stickam (now-defunct), the social network site based around live video chat, as a supplementary technology, maintaining consistent usernames across the two websites, and so effectively adding a 'plug-in' to YouTube. The use of Stickam amplified the social network affordances of YouTube and allowed the YouTubers to build their brands using ambient, 'always on' technology, rather than only through the production of static episodes of their vlogs. Such workarounds were necessary, given that the communities and subcultures who were making use of YouTube (Jenkins, 2009) pre-existed the platform, and were always already cross-platform, not contained within YouTube's architecture or technologies. When the video microblogging service 12seconds.tv launched in mid 2008, it similarly spawned a flurry of cross-registrations, resulting in a YouTube 'meme' built around twelve-second vlog entries.

Despite its ever-present community rhetoric, early YouTube's architecture and design invited individual participation, rather than collaborative activity. Any opportunities for collaboration had to be deliberately created by the YouTube community itself, or arose by special invitation from the company. Back in 2008, YouTube provided no built-in, routinised methods of capturing video from other users and reusing it, or of making one's own content available for this purpose. Nevertheless, collaborative and remixed vlog entries were a very noticeable feature of the most popular content in our survey. Sometimes, it was clear that a significant amount of planning had gone into the production of these videos and that they were attached to purposeful aims (like influencing the rankings, celebrating an event, and so on). At other times they appeared to function as ways of celebrating and representing YouTube as a community of practice. Within weeks of the launch of the 'microvlogging' site 12seconds.tv, which was designed as a plug-in to Twitter, several prominent YouTubers participated in a twelve-second collaborative vlog entry posted at 12seconds.tv and linked to from a longer, individually produced vlog entry by fantasticblabbings. Fantasticblabbings used the cross-post to discuss the proliferation of online identities across social network sites, expressing scepticism with regard to the faddish adoption and abandonment of these sites.[1] This provides an illustration of the extent to which YouTubers, as cultural agents, have never been fully captive to YouTube's architecture, and demonstrates the permeability of YouTube as a system. It connects with surrounding social and cultural networks, and users embedded within these networks move their content and their identities back and forth between multiple platforms. YouTube has never functioned as a closed system, from the beginning providing tools to embed content on other websites like blogs. By 2017, professional social media influencers or entertainers were operating in a dynamic, real-time, and cross-platform environment – working across a suite of popular social media platforms like Instagram, Twitter, Vine (now defunct), Twitch, and Snapchat, even if YouTube is 'home base'. This cross-platform model of practice amplifies the creative and relational labour required to maintain a successful presence, but it also reduces these creators' dependency on YouTube.

The early YouTubers engaged in a range of informal practices to make up for perceived lacks or missing affordances in the provided technology, which are of note especially where these go against the grain of the direction YouTube's business model was taking the platform. For example, interlinking and dialogical models of participation were part of the ideology and ethos of blogging, which was the dominant social media format of the early to mid 2000s. Many early YouTubers had already been successful bloggers and so expected the 'Flickr of video' to provide similar features. But even though the technologies needed to embed clickable links or user-contributed annotations and comments within video streams had existed for quite some time, up until mid 2008 no such capability had been introduced into YouTube, and the ability to refer back to other YouTube videos as part of each new utterance in a conversation was likewise very limited. Some of YouTube's competitors already offered the ability to tag and annotate other users' videos with comments, attached to various points in the video timeline. When YouTube did eventually add a video annotation feature, its use was limited to the owners of the videos (presumably to avoid an onslaught of annotation spam). YouTubers developed their own solution to the problem, collectively instituting conventions to work around the absence of true media richness and interactivity. In our 2007–8 study, we observed several instances where hyperlinks had been added as annotations in the texts of video descriptions or had been superimposed as graphics over the video footage, and then the performer physically pointed to the appropriate place on the screen to draw attention to the link. The collective development of manual solutions like this demonstrated the strong desire of the early YouTubers to embed their video practice within networks of conversation, rather than merely to 'broadcast themselves', and their willingness to find ways to do this even if not supported to do so by the provided technology.

Accessibility is another area in which the user community has played a major role. This is an important ongoing issue, especially as platforms like YouTube have become progressively less like websites and more like apps (and hence, less 'open' and hackable), even on the web. Because of its participatory character, YouTube has provided a platform for the formation of YouTube communities organised around disability activism in a range of contexts, including not only issues of media representation, but also in the context of the platform itself. While YouTube always wanted to make participation in online video available to 'everyone', the audiovisual turn and the reliance on the 'closed source' format of Flash video (a departure from web accessibility standards) created new web accessibility challenges.[2] YouTube videos themselves are less accessible to people with hearing disabilities unless closed captions are provided. Closed captions were first announced on the Google Video Blog in 2006 with a major overhaul (drawing on speech recognition technology to generate captions automatically) announced in 2009.[3] However, the quality of the automatically generated text, while improving, is notoriously terrible – so much so that auto-captions were lampooned in the popular YouTube series CAPTION FAIL – featuring videos that humorously act out the increasingly nonsensical song lyrics or scripts that emerge out of recursive auto-captioning (Ellcessor, 2016: 1–2). The technology itself has improved over time, but high levels of frustration remain, not only in regard to the low quality of auto-captions, but also to the low priority that closed captions seem to have with leading YouTubers and the platform. In 2016, prominent deaf YouTuber Rikki Poynter, who had already created a number of videos on the subject, started the viral hashtag campaign #nomorecraptions, which highlights nonsensical auto-caption 'fails' by posting screenshots or embedding YouTube videos on Twitter. Through the campaign, the deaf YouTube community called for YouTubers to write their own captions, thereby taking responsibility for accessibility of their content, rather than digitally delegating this task to the platform (Dupere, 2016). Deaf captioner Michael Lockrey developed a free tool to allow YouTube users to enter a YouTube URL, download, review, and then manually correct the caption file for the video, and re-publish with the improved captions;[4] and published educational materials for YouTubers interested in improving the captions that go with their videos, as well as updating the community on improvements to the platform's in-built auto-captioning feature.[5] This example shows, as Katie Ellis (2010) suggests, that there has been a co-influential relationship between disability activist communities on YouTube and a growing public understanding of the need for accessibility – in turn, making the platform more useful for everyone.

As this example shows, the community logics and social networking functions that have been part of YouTube's rhetoric from the beginning have also enabled creator communities to reflect, organise, and mobilise around their relationship to the platform and the company that provides it. Returning to the results of our original content survey, as a starting point, we conservatively estimated that a substantial proportion – at least 10 per cent – of the most popular YouTube videos uploaded between June and November 2007 were explicitly concerned with YouTube itself. Of these, more than 99 per cent were user-created; that is, almost none of these videos that were in some way *about* YouTube were coded as traditional media content. This finding is obvious in retrospect, because the mainstream media did not, as a rule, make much content specifically for YouTube in 2007, even though they were producing content destined generally for the web.

These user-created 'meta YouTube' videos (as we called them in our analysis) varied widely in their forms and modes of address, from collaborative montages that evoke a sense of community to simple slideshows using text and music that invite responses in a bid for popularity. Tellingly, a full two-thirds of these videos were vlog entries. In general, vlog entries implicitly address an audience of fellow YouTubers along with a wider imagined audience. One of the basic communicative functions of the vlog entry is purely phatic – it announces the social presence of the vlogger and calls into being an audience of peers who share the knowledge and experience of YouTube as a social space. But these specifically YouTube-focused vlog entries do something else as well: making videos about some aspect of YouTube demonstrates, and in fact requires, a reflexive understanding of how YouTube actually operates as a social network, rather than only as a distribution platform that can be used to broadcast to an online audience.

Throughout the platform's history, successful YouTubers have tended to be canny and knowledgeable about YouTube's attention economy, with all its many faults, and this knowledge is often performed playfully or humorously, even when their videos critique some aspect of the way the platform measures and rewards attention. The measures of popularity we discussed in the previous chapter have long been subject to gaming – even in 2008 there were companies that offered to send videos 'viral' for a fee; in 2017 the ancillary businesses attached to social media marketing are legion (Serazio and Duffy, 2017), and their use of astroturfing and automation techniques far more sophisticated. The early YouTube creator community was well aware of this – their discourse revealed a perceived link between the common characteristics of the most popular content (which seemed to them to represent an inauthentic overvaluation of sex, shock, and stupidity); and the actions that needed to be taken by content creators in order to gather and engage audiences. Some videos cheerfully exploited this knowledge of the value system of YouTube's common culture; some actively critiqued it. Whatever the perspective, these videos indicate that the most active participants in YouTube were highly knowledgeable – perhaps even more so, at that stage, than the company itself – of the specific ways in which these measures of popularity can work to support or disturb what they saw as the authentic, 'bottom-up' culture of YouTube, which they perceived as the source of the platform's value.

This mode of communication – performing insider knowledge in an entertaining way while also making interventions into the culture of the YouTube community – was evident in OhCurt's video 'Mission Improbable: An Almost Shout-Out',[6] which was one of the most discussed videos in our sample from 2007 (but is no longer available on the platform). The video was a collaborative vlog sketch in which OhCurt play-acted telephone conversations with the other YouTubers he was nominating in his response to yet another YouTuber's 'tell me five cool channels' invitation to mutual cross-promotion – a tradition that works to generate video replies and to create new connections between channels on the network. The humour of the sketch was based around farcical miscommunications and misunderstandings between YouTube participants, and gently parodied both the banality and attention-seeking logics of the 'shout-out' tradition – performing both insider expertise and irony.

Shout-out invitations are one example among many of the ways in which the self-constituting YouTube creator community introduces tactics to attempt to navigate, shape, and control the otherwise vast and chaotic array of content that exists in the network, as well as to generate attention and form new connections. The early YouTubers who participated in these ways were by definition 'lead users' (Von Hippel, 2005) – they were both early adopters of new technologies, ideas, and practices, and significant agents in the development of innovations that better serve the needs of the user community, and their knowledge was developed and situated in relation to that community. In order to operate effectively as a participant in YouTube (or any other digital media platform with its own 'vernaculars', conventions, and norms), it is never possible simply to import learned conventions for creative practice, and the cultural competencies required to enact them, from elsewhere (e.g. from professional television production).

The creation and performance of connections among YouTube channels – whether through shout-outs, plugs, or explicit collaborations on video production, have become embedded as important brand-building and audience engagement strategies for YouTube creators. While they are encouraged by MCNs (especially among channels that are part of the MCN's stable), they emerged out of this early YouTube culture, which in turn had antecedents in the network dynamics of the blogosphere and nascent pre-YouTube videoblogging community (Berry, 2015). Despite the increased complexity of its commercial ecosystem, 'success' for YouTubers of any size is still primarily measured according to the numbers and persistent engagement of subscribers who regularly return to watch and engage with a particular channel's content, thereby translating into attention for advertisers or brand sponsors. In order to succeed on these measures, YouTubers need to be able to understand and exploit the affordances of the platform (Postigo, 2016), as well as the platform-specific nature of community-building and audience engagement – and for those who have 'monetised', along the way building an 'advertiser-friendly' brand and consistent channel presence that serves YouTube's commercial interests as well.

## Learning with Others

Digital media literacy is one of the fundamental requirements of a more inclusive and diverse participatory culture. YouTube has always been the locus of both hope and concern about digital literacy, especially for young people. It is simultaneously a 'digital technology' (requiring new technical skills and knowledge); a new kind of 'media' platform, publishing a huge range of quasi-factual 'documentary' videos on the platform alongside (requiring 'critical media literacy'); and a platform where creative and 'maker' communities can form and interact (offering the potential for collective learning).

During the Web 2.0 moment of the mid 2000s, questions of literacy were in flux. Sonia Livingstone (2004) proposed then that most discussions of new media literacy were characterised by historically unresolved tensions between 'critical' or 'Enlightenment' views of literacy – polarised philosophical positions that see literacy as a normative and exclusionary construction on the one hand (the 'critical' view); or as an aid to progress and equality we should aim to extend to all people on the other (the 'Enlightenment' view). Proving Livingstone's point, the US media literacy movement has variously framed literacy as empowerment through, or therapy for the dangers of, the media (or both; see Hobbs, 1998). On the one hand, commentators suggested, young people might have been learning new media competencies through their participation in YouTube (Drotner, 2008); and at the same time, according to the media literacy framework, this active and creative participation might also be used to help young people learn to be more 'critical' of media messages (Jenkins et al., 2006). The definition developed by the UK media regulator Ofcom (and adopted extensively elsewhere) at around this time reflected this new emphasis on the interrelatedness of 'writing' as well as 'reading' competencies, as well as the convergence of information or ICT literacy with media literacy – it defined new media literacy as 'the ability to access, understand and create communications in a variety of contexts' (see Livingstone et al., 2008).

Our approach to the questions of literacy with respect to YouTube is closely aligned with the New Literacy Studies movement (Street, 1984; Knobel and Lankshear, 2014), where, instead of literacy being a 'technology of the mind' or set of skills (i.e. an internalised competency or range of competencies that can be attributed to or possessed by an individual human agent), it is considered a social practice. The most important outcome of these debates should be to understand that digital media literacy is not a property of individuals – something a given human agent either possesses or lacks – but a *system* that both enables and shapes participation. It still follows, however, that it is possible (and necessary) within this conceptual framework to talk about the individual competencies (or 'skills') required to participate effectively in this system. The questions of how this system is shaped and who has access to it represent the key political questions of digital literacy.

Since the mid 2000s, policy and practice around digital literacy have given more attention to both creativity and play; especially where these might connect to the development of design skills and coding competencies, as in the rise of Minecraft user communities – which have a strong presence on YouTube (Niemeyer and Gerber, 2015). Data literacy and social media platform literacy are rapidly becoming as important as content-centred or communicative literacies; often tied to privacy and online safety concerns. And information or news literacy is a fraught question that, in the era of concern about 'fake news', has only become more so – indeed, shortly after the 2016 US presidential election and amid the rise of the 'alt-right', danah boyd (2017) raised the question of whether media literacy – of the kind that teaches consumers to be critical of and aware of the political interests that sit behind the news – has 'backfired'; and that correctives such as information literacy or critical thinking programs are not likely to succeed, because it is empathy, understanding, and engaging across diverse experiences and modes of expertise that are most lacking and that societies most need to rediscover.

Being 'literate' in the context of YouTube, then, means not only being able to create and consume video content, but also being able to comprehend the way YouTube works as a platform, within an architecture that has affordances and constraints, and with a culture that has competing social and ethical norms and cultural conventions. For our purposes, what counts as 'literacy' is at least partly specific to the culture of YouTube itself. Individual competencies and knowledges are required, but not all of them can be imported from elsewhere. It is important to also note that, in our observations, while requiring a pre-existing familiarity with digital technologies and online culture, these competencies are not in-born natural attributes of the so-called digital natives (Prensky

2001a; 2001b). Indeed, many, if not most, of the most prominent early 'lead users' – those whose videos gained the most
attention and therefore those who were able to find an audience for their views or to mobilise other users – were adults
in their twenties or thirties who already had an online presence; that of course has changed since, with many famous
YouTubers who are kids and teens.

Peter Oakley, a British vlogger then in his eighties who was
known on YouTube as Geriatric1927, provides a good example of how YouTube-specific competencies can be learned and
mobilised through pro-social participation in the YouTube
community. Oakley was a consistently high-profile celebrity
on YouTube from its very early years, commencing in August
2006 and continuing until shortly before his death in 2014.[7]
His first videoblog post – a brief and tentative experiment
with a webcam and Windows Moviemaker humbly titled
'First Try', exploded onto the Most Viewed page of YouTube's
popularity rankings (largely because of the novelty, at the
time, of his age).[8] That first video had received more than
two-and-a-half million views by March 2008, rising to more
than three million by 2017. Oakley remained a regular and
very engaged member of the YouTube community, posting
on topics such as the making content for YouTube and the
ethics of online behaviour and 'haters'. By tracing his contributions to the website over time, we can see how Oakley used
his YouTube presence to reflect on and develop his own creative and technological competencies – progressing from basic
straight-to-camera vlogs using Windows Moviemaker to the
integration of photos with overlaid titles, and more complex
editing.

Geriatric1927 also become something of an evangelist. In
the video entry 'Computing for the Terrified',[9] Oakley records
himself carrying on a conversation over video chat with 'a
group of elderly residents living in sheltered accommodation
who are receiving instruction into basic computer techniques'.
Although we can only hear one side of the conversation,

Oakley is clearly reassuring and encouraging them to just 'have a go', using his own process of self-education as an example. He advises the participants in his workshop to 'just click around' or 'play a simple card game' to get the hang of the mouse until it's 'almost like a third hand', after which 'all sorts of amazing things will happen', and not to worry, because 'you really can't break a computer'. In fact, he says, 'you must be prepared to be a child again' – to learn by 'playing around'.

Oakley's videos made his own process of learning explicit through a process of reflection and communication – thus making his knowledge available to his peers. Further, the specific technological and cultural competencies that are required in order to navigate, communicate, and innovate within YouTube as a social network, as the example of Geriatric1927 demonstrates, are collectively constructed, taught, and learned as a part of participation in the YouTube community. Beyond functional digital media literacy, YouTube has always been a platform for peer learning about just about any subject, craft, or skill – guitar-playing, cooking, dancing, maths, plumbing, and computer games. Videos of players doing in-game stunts, compilations of in-game achievements, or illustrations of how to exploit glitches in games are about sharing knowledge as well as 'showing off' and showcasing one's own competencies, and of course the 'how-to' and gameplay genres are among the biggest sectors of commercial online video as at 2017.

## Controversies in the YouTube Community

As is the case elsewhere in digital culture, controversies regularly arise within the self-constituted communities of 'YouTubers', whether amateur or professionalising, around the politics of the uneven power relationship between the company and its users, and among different kinds of users. Such controversies are highly significant and analytically useful events: in the case of YouTube, they reveal the level of investment these users have in the platform and its cultures of use, the construction and characteristics of symbolic boundaries between the YouTubers as a core group of 'lead users' and an imagined 'mass' of ordinary users, and the ways these have changed over time. And as the business has commercialised, controversies have arisen over labour issues and the relationship between YouTube and its community of creators.

These controversies have revealed competing ideas about what YouTube is for – a social network site produced by communities of practice; a chaotic archive of weird, wonderful, and trashy vernacular video; or a distribution platform for branded and Big Media entertainment. Much of the discussion around these controversies centres around perceived changes to the culture of YouTube as it scales up, makes deals with major media players and attempts to create revenue from its constantly evolving business model. In participating in the debates around these controversies, the YouTubers exert an influence on a complex system to which, from their perspective, they collectively contribute much of the value, performing and protecting the considerable personal investments they have in the YouTube culture and community.

The activity that occurred around the launch of Oprah Winfrey's YouTube channel in early November 2007 was a particularly good example of the way participants in YouTube's social network use their own video channels to shape and contest the way the culture of YouTube is evolving. The launch was cross-promoted via a 'YouTube special' on the Oprah television show ('YouTube's Greatest Hits With The Billionaire Founders', 2007), in which a number of the current and all-time most viewed videos and their creators were featured as guest stars. It seemed to commenters that at some stage in that first week, the Oprah channel had been granted the privilege of editing the list of featured videos that appeared on the front page of the YouTube website, with the result being that the featured videos that week were predominantly (and approvingly) *about* Oprah in some way. There was an intense and immediate flurry of protest videos, spawning discussion about the implications of this event. One point made by several commentators was that Oprah was importing the convergence of celebrity and control associated with 'big media' into the social media space (by disallowing external embedding, by moderating comments) and therefore ignoring the cultural norms that have developed over the life of the network. The Oprah channel was seen as symptomatic of late-arriving corporate partners exploiting the market in attention that had been produced by earlier, more 'authentic', participants, a situation only exacerbated by YouTube's practice of proactively promoting their partnerships with mainstream media companies and celebrities who hadn't done the 'hard yards' in the subculture.

The blog devoted to YouTube, *YouTube Stars*, summed up the themes of the debates that occurred around this event:

> The YouTube community has reacted with ambivalence to Oprah's new channel. Some think it will bring new viewers for everyone's videos. But others object to Oprah's apparent 'one-way conversation' – she seems to want to advertise to us without accepting feedback. It has also been lamented that the 'golden age' of YouTube is over. With the corporate accounts racking up lots of viewers, it's hard to get on the most discussed or most viewed lists without resorting to histrionics and sensationalism. YouTube seemed more like a community of videomakers before 'partners' came on to advertise to us. But, all this was inevitable. YouTube was spending millions on the computer power and bandwidth necessary to provide this free service to the uploaders and viewers of the thousands of new videos posted weekly on the website.

In 'Noprah',[10] an entry from his humorous vlog, star YouTube comedian Nalts responded to the Oprah 'YouTube special' and her related move to establish a channel on YouTube. Nalts complained about the 'same old' videos, like the 'skateboarding dog', being used by 'Big Media' to represent YouTube. He voiced his irritation with Big Media not understanding the

YouTube 'community', as well as Oprah's own channel not allowing comments. Renetto, another A-list YouTuber and self-styled community leader, sarcastically commented that it was a good thing that Oprah got featured on the front page because, clearly, 'she has trouble broadcasting herself'.[11]

At around the same time, popular British vlogger Paperlilies argued in an entry entitled 'RIP the Golden Age of YouTube'[12] that the entrance of corporate players had produced a 'crazy playing field'. Asserting that her own videos are made 'in [her] bedroom', 'using iMovie', she proposed that YouTube needed to look at introducing new ways for visitors to navigate and find content that would allow people to find 'good' user-created content. She went on to express anxiety about the impact on the cultural ecology of YouTube of the company's recent success in attracting corporate partners:

> It felt like it was a community and it doesn't feel like that any-more. It feels like we're living in a TV channel and no-one's looking at us, we're just being trodden all over by corporate people who don't give a shit about the people who make videos.

There was a palpable sense of betrayal in these entries, along with the idea that the investment of time and effort the YouTube community has put in has gone unrewarded. This is not just a rights-based complaint motivated by jealousy or the loss of attention. Comments like these exhibit an ethic of care for the 'YouTube-ness' of YouTube, and an aspiration to preserve the unique and diverse flavour of 'bottom-up' participation. For Paperlilies and other 'lead' YouTubers, this is an issue of cultural diversity and sustainability, as much as one of mutual responsibility. She says, addressing the company:

> You've got the corporate thing now, you've got it down pat. Everyone wants to be on YouTube and that's great. But now you've got to go back to those people who made YouTube what it is, and promote them. Because a lot of people are feeling neglected by YouTube. And the site that they grew to love last summer is no more. Now we have just another TV

channel that happens to be on the Internet. And I don't like that.

Whereas it used to be that 'creative' or 'well-made' videos could get a 'huge amount of views', she said, now 'sensationalist' videos or those appealing to the 'lowest common denominator' get a lot of views, providing what the 'mainstream media' was providing before the emergence of YouTube. 'Creativity' (understood as innovative user-created content) is 'harder to find' the more content there is. As a postscript, by October 2017, Paperlilies had 67,700 subscribers but did not appear to be active. The channel description read 'I don't really make videos anymore, and I kinda hate youtube'.

At the same time, however, Blunty3000, another very well-known YouTuber who was still very active in late 2017,[13] expressed scepticism about the extent of the threat 'real celebrities' represent. He pointed out that the same debates occurred when Paris Hilton and P. Diddy got YouTube channels, occurrences which provoked a great deal of anxiety that later turned out to be unwarranted: 'Neither P. Diddy nor Paris Hilton really affected the YouTube community in any way, shape or form'. Blunty also argued that Oprah's cross-promotion of her own YouTube presence would have the unintended consequence of bringing new audiences, not to the Oprah brand, but also to *user-created* YouTube content. In the end, Oprah is 'just another YouTuber', he concludes, but one who may significantly expand the audience, hence benefiting the community as a whole; and, in fact, the protest videos themselves could be seen as a way of cashing in on the Oprah brand, diverting the resultant attention back toward the YouTubers themselves.

The controversy around Oprah's entrance to YouTube, then, functioned partly as an opportunity for the community to reflect explicitly on, take stock of, and activate around the terms of participation within which they were working. These videos were also part of a much longer-term and more widespread pattern of community 'protest' videos, frequently led by the more well-known YouTubers. In her vlog entry entitled 'YouTube is NOT involved with the Community', vlogger xgobobeanx (whose re-branded channel Jill Hanner is still active)[14] discussed a number of perceived inadequacies and inequities in YouTube's community management practices. Her description of the video expressed irritation that 'YouTube does not answer emails and that anyone can flag a video without any notice or explanation. Why do partners get away with so much?' Much of the argument is grounded in a separation between (media) partners on the one hand, and 'the community' (non-corporate 'YouTubers') on the other. The content of this distinction makes less sense in the age of the highly monetised star YouTubers, but the process of making the distinction – a social one – is just as meaningful to the discursive maintenance of community logics. The importance of this distinction is also illustrated by some of the counter-tactics employed by the YouTube community to gain some control over the public landscape of the website. For example, the website *YouTube Stars* regularly published a chart of the 'Non Corporate Top 100' YouTube videos, which was similar to YouTube's Most Viewed videos page, but with all content uploaded by known corporate partners filtered out.[15]

This resistance to the perceived commercial appropriation of grass-roots enterprise is not unique to YouTube, of course. It is very similar to the perception of 'appropriation' or 'selling out' that has been so well documented in relation to music subcultures and scenes that go from being marginal to the mainstream (see, for example, Schilt, 2003, on the Riot Grrrl phenomenon in the 1990s). Protesting, parodying, or participating in the turbulence around the perceived transformation of YouTube from DIY free-for-all to corporate media platform has been a way of performing insider knowledge and expertise during each new phase of mainstreaming or commercialisation. The discourse that takes places around these controversies reveals the tensions between the 'active' participants, or 'core users', who play by the rules that have been collectively established over time by the user community, and those who, according to the perceptions of the YouTubers, contribute to the erosion of the cultural value and integrity of the service by disregarding those norms: haters (who haven't uploaded their own videos but leave abusive comments in the discussion threads of other users' videos); big media players (like Oprah) who assume the privileges of cultural authority without earning them on the ground; and YouTube the company, who simply rewrites the rules in their own interests. These discussions and controversies reveal the shared but implicit understanding of the social contract between the YouTubers and the company. This implicit understanding might only be made explicit once it appears to be disrupted by new developments (like the Oprah channel's launch in 2007, or the 'adpocalypse' in 2017, discussed in the concluding chapter), at which time discourses of entitlement, fairness, and labour emerge.

As well as revealing the emerging politics of the relationships between the YouTube user community, YouTube Inc., and big media organisations, the controversies and debates that can be observed via YouTube vlog entries also concern the norms of behaviour within the YouTube community and the political divisions within it. It is well known that there are issues in YouTube with abusive comments, exacerbated by anonymity (so that there are few disincentives to behave badly) and scale (so that it becomes difficult to keep up with policing and moderating comments). YouTube has introduced various mechanisms to help deal with abusive and harmful comments. These have ranged from user ratings systems; algorithmic curation of comments by 'relevance' rather than in chronological order, combined with human moderators working behind the scenes; an attempted push toward the use of real names in 2012 – which also would have required YouTube users to log in with their Google Plus usernames and hence became entangled in the 'nymwars', which is shorthand for Google's much larger fight with Google Plus users over the right to pseudonymity (Galperin, 2011); and more recently the 2016 introduction of the YouTube Heroes program, an enhanced community moderation system where only trusted users have the power to flag comments (Kastrenakes, 2016).

To an extent, the apparently antisocial communicative practices of trolls and haters had already become normalised in YouTube's culture, and quite early in its history, at least for the most popular videos. Many prominent YouTubers historically have expressed reluctance to moderate or ban comments because those kinds of controls are counter to the ethos of openness that supposedly distinguishes participatory culture. Lange (2007a) explains that dealing with the 'haters' – negative and often personally offensive commenters – is part of the YouTube experience for those who participate in YouTube as a social network, and something YouTubers accept as part of the game, taking the bad with the good. Learning how to 'manage' trolls, both practically and emotionally, is one of the core competencies required for effective or enjoyable participation. Anthony McCosker (2014) also points out that some forms of passionate, antagonistic engagement can actually be seen as forms of citizenship, because they provoke the emergence of publics around a topic.

As always, diverse YouTube communities have found their own ways of negotiating and shaping the social norms of the platform. In our original study, in the collaborative video 'Being a Chick on YouTube',[16] a male and female YouTuber discussed the implications of the sexist and often abusive comments that prominent female YouTubers have to contend with. The video demonstrates a sophisticated knowledge of the issue – rather than moralising about it, the two participants in the video discussed the possible negative impact of this culture of sexism on the participation rates of female vloggers. Cleverly, it addressed the assumed motivations of the male audience, arguing that the development of an overly masculinist and sexist culture among the YouTube community would result in a scarcity of female YouTubers with whom to interact. From the beginning, YouTubers have explicitly tried to shape social norms and reflexively negotiate the ethics of online behaviour, operating from a position of grounded, insider knowledge.

But in the English-speaking Internet of 2017, trolling is organised, community moderation is subverted, and comments are weaponised as part of deliberate and organised strategies to silence people of colour, women, sexual minorities, and progressive voices (Phillips, 2015). The events surrounding the 2014–15 #gamergate controversy and related social media activity brought the darker aspects of online trolling into the mainstream, and YouTube was a significant site of #gamergate activity, with organised campaigns of harassment against leading progressive and female gamers mounted on the platform (Burgess and Matamoros-Fernández, 2016). Since then, the far-right activity leading up to the 2016 US presidential election and increasingly emboldened since then has dramatically heightened the perception of how important it is for platforms to deal with misinformation and abuse (Marwick and Lewis, 2017). Effective community governance of behaviour and content relies on good faith, both in the user community and in the platform. It is not possible to assume good faith in the YouTube community when it is populated by trolls and sock puppets as well as earnest amateurs and media professionals; and it is just as difficult to assume good faith in platforms (like YouTube, Twitter, and Facebook) whose metrics and algorithms are opaque and appear to reward attention above all else. In such times, effective community governance is more difficult than ever to achieve, but achieving it has never been more urgent.

A different variety of conflict and antagonism in the YouTube community is the 'flame war' or 'YouTube drama' – which should be thought of separately from the general carelessness or nefarious mischief-making of casual commenters or 4Chan trolls. These events occur when a flurry of video posts clusters around an internal 'controversy' or an antagonistic debate between one or more YouTubers. They can sometimes be based around controversial debates (especially religion, atheism, or politics). But quite often they appear as face-offs between YouTube stars based around the internal politics and power plays of the YouTube community itself. These short-lived, but very intense, community events are often engaged in playfully – they function as entertainment as much as debates and discussions. Indeed, flame wars can be thought of as ludic events: structured games that are part of the fun of participating on the platform.

A good example of this from the period in which our content survey took place was the controversy over prominent user Lisa Donovan (whose original username and current channel name is LisaNova)[17] allegedly 'spamming' others with comments in order to attract audiences to her channel. It was quite evident that, as part of the controversy playing itself out, the trolling, hating, and parodying became spectacles in themselves. This classic YouTube drama also revealed the internal tensions between the very small number of YouTubers who have become highly successful in the Partner Program, and the larger group of core YouTubers. The occasional antagonisms between 'A-list' YouTubers and the rest of the 'core' user group were partly a result of the monetisation of popularity; the success of the YouTube 'stars' is an element of the perception that YouTube has been evolving from a community-driven platform to a more mainstream, commercial space. Donovan is indeed paradigmatic of an early YouTuber who became a key player in the new commercial sphere of multi-platform entertainment – she successfully made the crossover into TV and movies as a comedy actor, and was a co-founder of prominent multi-channel network Maker Studios.

At issue in these controversies is the extent to which

YouTubers (whether partners or not) have an influence on the future of the community in which they have so much investment. Most significantly, they provide an indication of the competing logics of expertise, authority, and value that are at work within YouTube as a cultural space. The controversies also help us to understand how participation in this self-constituted YouTube 'community' relies on various forms of vernacular expertise, combining a critical and literate under-standing of the 'attention economy' and the affordances of the network with the ability to navigate the social and cultural norms of the community. Of course, drama is an animating cultural dynamic of the YouTube 'community' – it at once reinforces the idea of co-present participants in a social world, and reinscribes the competitive market logics of professional-ising YouTubers (Cunningham and Craig, 2017). And, just as Hollywood has celebrity gossip columnists, there is a whole sub-genre of videoblogging specifically devoted to reporting on ongoing YouTube dramas and digging up dirt on them through investigative reporting, as YouTuber-centric publica-tion *We the Unicorns* has discussed (Kolaki, 2017).

Despite its internal antagonisms, performances of irony, and inauthentic authenticity, it is the YouTube community, pro-duced out of interactions between participants via their videos, that provides the environment in which new literacies, new cultural forms, and new social practices – situated in and appro-priate to the culture of user-created online video – have been originated, adopted, and retained (Potts et al., 2008a). Before there were millionaire YouTubers, MCNs, and YouTube TV, it was the participants in early YouTube who produced much of the platform's cultural, social, and economic value, and who fostered its iconic cultural forms and genres. Star YouTubers have evolved a set of practices and norms out of this early his-tory that incorporate the need to balance authenticity, intimacy, and community, but also take it forward in complex commer-cial arrangements with brands, and fraught relationships with both the MCNs and the platform itself.

# CHAPTER FIVE

# YouTube's Cultural Politics

In this chapter we explore the ways that YouTube has generated public and civic value as an unintended and often unsupported consequence of the practices of its diverse and global users, and the ongoing tensions between these value-generating practices and the changing business model and regulatory structures of the platform. The chapter is divided into three sections. The first section explores the affordances and limitations of YouTube for cultural citizenship and cultural diversity. The second section traces the transformation of YouTube from a globally interconnected platform on the 'borderless' Internet to a more re-localised one. The final section highlights the value of YouTube as an accidental archive, and the cultural policy and implications of this both for YouTube and for institutions of public memory like libraries. Reflecting on changes and evolution of the platform over its life so far, we argue that the larger in scale and demographic reach YouTube has become, the more that is at stake in terms of public value, highlighting the policy and regulatory challenges of the commercial platform paradigm.

## Diversity and Cultural Citizenship

YouTube is, and has always been, a commercial enterprise. But it has also always been a platform designed to enable cultural participation by ordinary people. Despite all the complexity of its professional media ecology, the inclusiveness and openness of the YouTube promise that 'anyone' can participate is also fundamental to its distinctive commercial value proposition. This is what we mean when we say that, for YouTube, *participatory culture is core business*. It is a highly visible example of the broader trend toward uneasy convergences of market and non-market modes of cultural production in the digital environment, where marginal, subcultural, and community-based modes of cultural production are by design incorporated within the commercial logics of major media corporations. As we have already suggested, YouTube's value is partly generated out of the collective creativity and communication of its users and audiences, and its culture has both commercial and community motivations and outcomes. Because of this, YouTube has provided a platform for participation in digital media culture for a much broader range of participants than before, and indeed its brand trades on the social and cultural diversity of the voices it supports.

From a media and cultural studies perspective, access to and participation in popular culture is an important means to political participation and citizenship, especially for women, LGBTQ people, and religious or ethnic minorities (Hartley, 1999; Hermes, 2005, 2006). Here, citizenship is defined not only as a matter of an individual's codified rights and obligations in relation to the state, but also in terms of how individuals participate in practices and collectives that form around matters of shared interest, identity, or concern. Joke Hermes (2005) suggests that notions of citizenship 'can also be used in relation to less formal everyday practices of identity construction, representation, and ideology, and implicit moral obligations and rights' (2005: 4), defining 'cultural citizenship' as:

> the process of bonding and community building, and reflection on that bonding, that is implied in partaking of the text-related practices of reading, consuming, celebrating, and criticising offered in the realm of (popular) culture. (2005: 10)

Popular cultural texts and practices, she writes, are important because 'they provide much of the wool from which the social tapestry is knit'. Karina Hof (2006: 364) uses these ideas in a study of scrapbooking communities, arguing that 'scrapbooking exemplifies how an everyday cultural practice can magnetise and mobilise people through a community of practice'. Participation in both scrapbooking as an individual creative practice and in communities of practice that form around scrapbooking, Hof argues, 'offers a very visible form and forum through which scrappers show what and whom they care about, how they live and where they fit into society at large' (2006: 364). Not only that, but such cultural participation also entails the exercising of 'duties and privileges' (the practice of cultural citizenship). This model of cultural citizenship could just as easily apply to the creation, showcasing, and discussion of video content in YouTube, within communities of interest.

Given its multinational provenance, YouTube also provokes questions about the relationship between the individual and a global, culturally diverse idea of community, involving both shared experiences and encounters with difference. Such questions have been the focus of scholarly debates in Internet and communication studies since the 1990s, which was a period of significant media change involving the fragmentation of traditional broadcast and print media and the gradual increase in take-up of the Internet and the World Wide Web. Foreshadowing the social media age, which is marked by personalisation and algorithmic content curation, Gandy (2002: 458) argued that the 'real digital divide' was the result of a social shaping of new media toward the interests of already powerful social groups, marked by class-specific characteristics, including profound individualisation. In the late 1990s, Michael Tracey (1998: 263) framed this social shaping as a barrier to what had been traditionally understood as a democratic public sphere – creating a mediated social world that is 'profoundly individualistic and definitely not collective, public, shared, or coherent'. For Tracey, increased 'relevance' and personalisation of content around our individual interests and the proliferation of 'niche markets' do not necessarily result in a more democratic participatory culture, regardless of whether the culture is produced by individuals or corporations. However, Nick Stevenson (Stevenson, 2003a; 2003b) argued that it was possible to imagine a progressive, cosmopolitan cultural citizenship despite the reality of our increased individualisation, if only we could better promote sustained opportunities for participation and dialogue, requiring the genuine negotiation of complexity and difference.

This earlier, optimistic idea that an ever-more commercialised and professionalised platform organised around entertainment – whatever the source of its content – could contribute to such worthy ideals (particularly given the political climate in much of the English-speaking and European world in 2017) is not as far-fetched as it might at first appear. Indeed, it is because so much of the symbolic material mediated via YouTube originates in the everyday lives of ordinary citizens, or is evaluated, discussed, and curated by them, that YouTube, in theory, represents a site of cosmopolitan cultural citizenship. But the communicative practices that constitute this form of cultural citizenship are more frequently found very far down the 'long tail' from the more professional, spectacular, or antagonistic mode of participation associated with YouTube's most visible popular culture, which was the subject of Chapter 3. Far from the dizzying heights of 'social media entertainment' stardom or trolling subcultures, the platform remains a mediator and connector of activities that might be recognised by scholars of popular culture as the practices of cultural citizenship – mundane but engaging activities that create spaces for engagement and community formation. Models of participation that function in this way range from peer-to-peer guitar lessons to 'memes' based around everyday consumption, where a large number of YouTube participants respond in video form to questions like 'What's in your fridge?';[1] as well as genuinely empathetic spaces for identity-based communities and for the sharing of personal stories.

Patricia Lange (2007c, n.p.) notes that even though

> people who are unfamiliar with the diary form of video blog-
> ging are often critical of this genre, seeing it as centred and
> obsessed with filming micro-events with no particular point
> or relevance beyond the videomaker's own life ... many
> video bloggers argue that it is precisely by putting these inti-
> mate moments on the Internet for all to see that a space is
> created to expose and discuss difficult issues and thereby
> achieve greater understanding of oneself and others.

Drawing on her ethnographic interviews with early (mainly women) videobloggers, Lange argued that 'public access to intimate moments and the discourse surrounding the video artifacts on the Web allow social boundaries and pre-existing assumptions to be questioned and refashioned', therefore converting the interpersonal and intimate identity work of everyday life to articulate to more 'public' debates around social identities, ethics, and cultural politics. In contrast to the spectacular flame wars between atheists and theists that were frequently a feature of our sample of the most popular content in 2007, Lange described a case in her study, in which 'the quiet, intimate, yet public exploration of feelings about atheism set in motion by a private conversation with a coworker prompted a reconsideration of how personal views may transform into political questions'. In these quiet moments of communication facilitated via, but not contained within, the video blog as 'text', Lange saw hope for an enrich-ment of public discourse: 'by being vulnerable and sharing intimate moments and choices, it is possible to promote increased public discourse about formerly uncomfortable, dis-tasteful, or difficult topics in ways that other media and other methods have not'.

Even though YouTube has become ever-more commercial, these deeply personal and social practices have remained an important part of it for some participants. YouTube in 2017 is no less immediate and intimate for those who use it as a social medium than it was for those early adopters with whom Lange worked. Margaret Gibson (2015) has conducted extensive research on online mourning, and her article on 'bereavement vlogging', which explores the practice of videoblogging about personal bereavement resulting in video blogs with very high levels of immediacy and intimacy, demonstrates that for some YouTube participants the platform is primarily, not secondarily social. This finding is thoroughly supported by Tobias Raun's (2016) extensive and in-depth study of trans video bloggers, which traces the way that participation in YouTube works both to build community and to enhance community-led forms of media representation and activism.

In particular, 'coming out' videos have become particularly significant 'social media rituals' (Burgess, Mitchell, and Münch, 2018) for LGBTQ YouTubers. The creation and sharing of coming out videos is a practice which precedes but was amplified by the It Gets Better Project (Johnson, 2014; Gal et al., 2016) – a video meme established by Dan Savage and amplified by youth-oriented broadcast and cable media including MTV and Glee. The meme format features mostly LGBTQ adults sharing stories of difficulties experienced in their teen years (including with homophobic bullying) – and the stories of how they overcame this. While the project itself has received criticism (including for its lack of diversity), the format's reliance on intense intimacy and personal storytelling is part of YouTube's DNA – both as a social media platform and as a commercial media business. The memetic, iterative qualities of the project also enable the community to reflect and critique the original concept and format, incorporating the possibility of more radical queer perspectives (Gal et al., 2016).

The role of YouTube in social connection and community activism is not restricted to participation in personal videoblogging, however; and it can operate in very subtle ways. The quoting of traditional media content we discussed in Chapter 3 also constitutes a very ordinary way in which citizens participate in and constitute communities or publics.

Constructing meaning through redaction can work to serve similar purposes – delineating, articulating, and expressing particular identities and modes of engagement with the world as members of particular communities; in early YouTube, sports and anime fandoms provided particularly vibrant examples. For example, some of the quoted material in our sample featured footage from soccer matches, edited to include pictures of fans, and details of their adventures following certain teams throughout the season. Videos such as these gave material form and visibility to the identities of fans as members of a community of fellow enthusiasts. Uploading this material served as a way for the group to talk among themselves, and to the broader community, using the same media texts that brought them together. So too, the uploading of Filipino or Turkish soap opera episodes, divided into pieces to get around YouTube's earlier content limits, can be seen as acts of cultural citizenship akin to the media-sharing practices of diasporic communities identified by Cunningham and Nguyen (2000).

YouTube remains a potential enabler and amplifier of cosmopolitan cultural citizenship – a space in which individuals can represent their identities and perspectives, engage with the self-representations of others, and encounter cultural difference. But access to all the layers of possible participation is shaped by the platform's cultural logics and affordances; and it depends on the motivations, technological competencies, and site-specific cultural capital sufficient to participate at all levels of engagement the network affords. Further, access to voice is no guarantee of an empathetic or engaged audience (Couldry, 2006) – listening, too, is a cultural competency that is necessary to social cohesion. Therefore, there are deep links between so-called 'filter bubbles' or 'echo chambers' (the failure of systems to expose users to difference), and the problem of digital inclusion, related to what Henry Jenkins called the 'participation gap' (Jenkins, 2006a: 258; Jenkins et al., 2006). This is why both digital literacy and diverse and inclusive online communities – even leisure or entertainment-based ones – are such important issues for politics.

While the affordances of the technologies and media forms associated with the participatory turn have increased the number and diversity of producers, and undoubtedly moved a significant number of people toward cultural production, the question of audience engagement *for diversity* – and what platforms can or should be doing to encourage and shape that engagement, rather than only rewarding the loudest voices, is urgent. YouTube is proud of its diversity and progressive social change initiatives like its Creators for Change program, which connects diverse, international YouTubers with progressive causes and with each other.[2] But as discussed in the previous chapter, its logics of popularity and how they are expressed as metrics – as is the case with Facebook's newsfeed – may continue to reward noise and controversy over all else.

## Globalisation and Localisation

A decade of change – involving intermediation and disintermediation, globalisation and localisation, social discovery and algorithmic personalisation (Burgess, 2015) – has left open the question of whether YouTube enables a more cosmopolitan media environment (where we can encounter surprising new perspectives) or ever-shrinking 'filter bubbles' (where our existing taste preferences, social worlds, and opinions are catered for and reinforced) (Flaxman et al., 2016). The competing dynamics of globalisation and localisation are a particularly important aspect of this.

Stewart Butterfield, co-founder of the photosharing website Flickr, once encapsulated the corporate vision for the erstwhile Web 2.0 success story in the phrase 'the eyes of the world':

> That can manifest itself as art, or using photos as a means of keeping in touch with friends and family, 'personal publish-

ing' or intimate, small group sharing. It includes 'memory preservation' (the de facto understanding of what drives the photo industry), but it also includes the ephemera that keeps people related to each other: do you like my new haircut? should I buy these shoes? holy smokes – look what I saw on the way to work! It lets you know who's gone where with whom, what the vacation was like, how much the baby grew today, all as it's happening . . . And most dramatically, Flickr gives you a window into things that you might otherwise never see, from the perspective of people that you might otherwise never encounter. (Butterfield, 2006)

Butterfield's explanation links together individual consumption, social intimacy, and everyday creativity with global intercultural communication – all based around sharing personal photographs. If Flickr aimed to be the 'eyes of the world', was YouTube destined to be the eyes *and* the ears? YouTube is 'global' in the sense that the Internet is – it is accessible from (almost) anywhere in the world, a feature that brings it into conflict with the content filtering and media control frameworks of a number of nations. It is also *globalising* in that it allows virtual border crossings between the geographical location of producers, distributors, and consumers.

In 2007, when we embarked on our survey of YouTube's most popular content, there was a single, global YouTube. In June of the same year, shortly after we had completed data collection, the platform began rolling out localised versions (Suciu, 2007), beginning with Brazil, France, Ireland, Italy, Japan, the Netherlands, Poland, Spain, and the UK, each with country-specific domain names (like youtube.br for Brazil). By mid 2008 there were different versions of YouTube being pushed out into Germany, Australia, Canada, the UK, Ireland, New Zealand, Spain, Mexico, France, Italy, China, Japan, the Netherlands, Poland, Brazil, Russia, Hong Kong, and Taiwan; by 2017 there were ninety different country versions. At first, upon visiting the YouTube website, users could opt for a localised version by selecting from a localisation menu with the options represented by the flags of each country for which a localised version was available. Content was customised for location, returning search results that were deemed more 'relevant' to the user based on their geographic location, as well as providing country-specific video rankings and comments. As at April 2008, users could choose the particular country version they wished to view, but they could also choose a language separately, meaning any country's version of the website could be viewed in any of the available languages. It was also possible to leave the country designation 'global', the default designation for the United States. As YouTube consumption increasingly went mobile, the apps and eventually the website defaulted to displaying content filtered for the user's location. In September 2017, visiting the YouTube.com homepage from an Australian location results in a local version, with only a small 'AU' annotation above the redesigned YouTube logo in the top right-hand corner of the page to give it away. As at October 2017 it is possible to customise both the default language and the content location by going to user account settings and then scrolling to the bottom of the page[3] – but this won't allow users to get around the geo-restriction of content that is a result of licensing arrangements that YouTube has struck with content owners with respect to various international markets.

In our original 2008 study, community responses to the introduction of localisation were sparse and largely indifferent, and protest videos relating to the move were quite difficult to find. The dominant line of complaint was that some countries weren't yet included in the program, so that their experience defaulted to another country – a complaint that came mainly from English-speaking countries such as Australia and Canada, who resented being included as an extension of the UK or the US. Those who did protest not only resented having to choose between either the UK flag or the US one (which, until uproar prompted the company to revert to a 'globe' symbol, was used to represent the 'default', global version of the website), but also felt moved to demand a version of YouTube localised for their own countries, in a kind of 'me too-ism'. Indeed, in the period during which the original research for this book was undertaken, the only prominent controversy that came close to addressing the issues of cultural diversity and globalisation in relation to company decisions was around YouTube's composition of a 'Community Council' that only comprised white participants. Even then, though, the fact that the 'community council' was also dominated by North Americans appeared to escape the notice of most of the participants in this debate.

In Segev, Ahituv, and Barzilai-Nahon's (2007) comparative study of MSN and Yahoo! homepages across various local markets, they quite presciently argued that it was equally important to be concerned about US website visitors encountering less 'global' content as it was to be concerned about the dominance of local websites with US content. From the point of view of cultural politics, it is questionable whether localisation is a good thing for cosmopolitan cultural citizenship, which requires the genuine encounter with difference. Indeed, under such criteria, because of their 'introverted' mode of engagement with the outside world (Rose, 2005), perhaps US-based YouTube participants needed a *globalised* YouTube far more than the rest of the world needs a 'localised' one. While US and other English-speaking users are introverted language users and cultural consumers, Richard Rose argues that speakers of languages other than English are generally more cosmopolitan, which, he suggests, adds up to a significant and growing form of 'soft power' in the context of globalisation.

Since then, around the world local YouTube 'scenes' have emerged, both organically and with YouTube's influence and with the participation of talent-hungry MCNs (for the example of YouTube in India, where it connects both to the entertainment ecology and vernacular politics, see Kumar, 2016; Punathembekar, 2015). But, overall, localisation has been part of a general trend away from chaotic networked cosmopolitanism and toward a fragmentation and re-territorialisation of the Internet through the platformisation of social media, bringing with it personalisation and localisation, all trends to which Google/YouTube have contributed. Beyond the huge stars and breakout international viral hits like Gangnam Style (interpreted as little more than an exotic Asian novelty in the West), this has made it increasingly unnecessary for Western, English-speaking users to encounter mundane cultural difference in their experience of online video.

Of course, localisation may bring with it easier compliance with particular national legal and regulatory frameworks – a consistent source of corporate headaches for both YouTube and its parent company Google/Alphabet. YouTube is unavailable in China and has been periodically banned in Turkey for political reasons; other countries with strong local content traditions and advanced digital cultures, especially in East Asia, have generally rejected US social media, and so YouTube has made little impact on them at all, despite aggressive marketing attempts on behalf of the company. Like other big content intermediaries, including Google and social media platforms like Facebook, YouTube balances its own business interests (which include global expansion) with a range of competing national regulatory structures while at the same time maintaining a brand image based on universal accessibility, and ideologically embedded in a particularly US-centric ideology of free speech. Tensions arise around the need to control which 'markets' certain content is accessed in (primarily an issue for corporate content providers like music labels and television networks) or to navigate the content regulation and censorship regimes of particular states – for example, to comply with the very strong regulation around hate speech and neo-Nazi imagery in Germany. One of the ways these tensions are resolved is through the selective use of content-specific geo-local filters. Further complications are added by the need for advertiser-friendliness, not only for those channels whose videos are monetised, but for the platform as a whole.

YouTube has progressively introduced a range of content filtering and take-down policies enacted through increasingly automated technologies, effectively shaping and reshaping the global cultural public sphere, but with no systematic, mandated responsibility to disclose the details of, or reasoning behind, these decisions. As users, we are generally none the wiser, instead being suddenly confronted by mysteriously inaccessible videos and incomplete search results, accompanied by nothing more than enigmatic messages like 'this video is not available in your country', or just, 'this video is unavailable'. New forensic digital methods that can enable researchers to identify patterns in take-downs and geo-local filters, and increasing policy pressure for transparency, may have an impact on this issue; but platform governance is an increasingly significant challenge across all digital and social media platforms.

## YouTube as Cultural Archive

When we ask adults, 'What do you watch on YouTube?', they will often tell us that they spend hours at a time watching old music videos, half-forgotten TV commercials, or clips from *Sesame Street* – recapturing memories from their childhood or young adulthood, navigating through related videos or keyword searches, often discovering media moments they thought had been lost forever. We know that the majority of YouTube audiences go there for music, but 76% of them are consuming music they are already familiar with, rather than making new discoveries (McIntyre, 2017). This points us toward an important and widespread alternative use of YouTube, but one that is less frequently featured in discussions of its implications: the use of YouTube as a cultural archive.

It is possible to exhaust your own capacity for nostalgia

before exhausting the possibilities of the vintage material available on YouTube already. Major music labels have added to the archival depth by contributing videos from their back catalogues (while at the same time forcing fan uploads off the platform), and cable or free-to-air channels such as HBO, the BBC, and the Australian Broadcasting Corporation are uploading material from the vault, as well as regularly using the platform to cross-promote current programming. But the bulk of YouTube's massive and diverse archive of cultural ephemera – vintage advertisements, infomercials and public educational materials, documentary films, and clips from children's shows – have been made available as the result of hours of painstaking labour, undertaken by the amateur collectors and curators of television who are digitising video tapes in their garages, editing them for upload at YouTube, tagging and describing them, and arranging them into channels or playlists. Even without the contributions of these pro-am collectors, archivists, and curators, whose practices contribute to building YouTube as a cultural archive, it has evolved into one as an unintended consequence of how it is used. Indeed, YouTube's status as an archive is more consistent with the platform's now-abandoned 'Your Digital Video Repository' tagline than their residually infamous (and now also defunct) provocation to 'Broadcast Yourself'.

The collective activities of thousands of users, each with their individual enthusiasms and eclectic interests, have created a living archive of contemporary culture from a large and diverse range of sources. YouTube users are actively engaged in the preservation and archiving of their own history – memorialising retired or deceased videobloggers, and producing montage after montage of now-classic viral videos. YouTube is not only a repository of vintage video content, but something even more significant: a living and growing record of the popular culture of the Internet. It has evolved into a massive, heterogeneous, but for the most part accidental and disordered, and increasingly precarious, public archive.

This idea of YouTube as an archive has significance for cultural heritage, supplementing the more specifically purposeful and highly specialised practices of state-based cultural archiving institutions like public libraries and museums; or media companies and broadcasters, whose role has transformed and who have become increasingly engaged in end-user engagement and crowdsourcing activities. Writing in a journal devoted to librarianship studies, Karen F. Gracy (2007) was early to consider the implications of YouTube as an unfiltered, bottom-up cultural archive for the role cultural institutions play:

> If cultural institutions no longer muster the same authority to curate collections – and by curate I mean shape them through the activities of acquisition, appraisal, description, deaccessioning, and all the other processes in which such institutions engage – what is their role within society and in regard to cultural heritage? (Gracy, 2007: 184)

Alan Mckee's (2011) comparative analysis of YouTube and the Australian National Film and Sound Archive found that both offered deep historical archives of key moments in Australian television, but that YouTube captured what we might consider to be a 'people's archive', focusing on key narrative moments and characters, whereas the official institution collected according to its own institutional logics. The implication is that there is definitely room for both institutional and popular archives, and that professional archivists, librarians and curators (as well as public service broadcasters) should be supported to work within or alongside YouTube to achieve their organisational missions.

On the other hand, far less consideration has been given to the implications of commercial spaces taking on some of the functions of cultural institutions (even as an unintended consequence or side-benefit) without being tied to the same public and state-based responsibilities. Archivist Rick Prelinger (2007) argues that those who have provided the infrastructure which has unexpectedly produced these accidental archives, as in the case of YouTube, are mostly 'blithely unconcerned by [the] questions of persistence, ownership, standards, sustainability, or accountability' that occupy professional archivists and their parent institutions. Because YouTube offers its service based on commercial interests, rather than public ones, there is no obligation to store these data beyond the commercial viability of the company that provides the storage service. As Robert Gehl (2009) has argued, in YouTube the platform architecture is not organised around this purpose. Indeed, given the triumph of copyright logics, in some cases the platform architecture and protocols actively work against the possibility of archiving, particularly for the videos themselves.

Such challenges are among the motivations for the development of the far broader Internet Archive project and its 'Wayback Machine', which is an attempt to gather, store, and make available iterative historical 'snapshots' of as many websites as possible. The Wayback Machine has been a godsend in the preparation of this book and many other Internet and platform studies projects – but its functionality and usefulness are increasingly challenged by rich media content and dynamic web technologies: YouTube as a platform compounds the already-significant methodological challenges of Web History (Brügger, 2017). Nor is there any straightforward way cultural institutions like the Library of Congress or equivalents in other countries can re-archive material that shows up on YouTube, because of legal barriers such as copyright law, and YouTube's Terms of Use. While archiving popular and media culture is significant in its own right, the importance of this challenge has been driven home by the role that YouTube eyewitness video has played in documenting conflict and human rights abuses, and the significance that uneven (or deliberately reshaped) collective memory can have for history and for justice (Smit et al., 2017). Relatedly, YouTube's Community Guidelines (operationalised through a combination of machine learning and manual flagging and removal) frequently see the take-down of violent or otherwise 'inappropriate' content that could have historical significance, and therefore their removal could 'impede justice', as *Wired*'s Scott Edwards has argued (2017). This was the case with footage of the Syrian conflict which was removed by YouTube after being flagged as violent, and – following protests and consultation with human rights groups – later restored (O'Brien, 2017). But of course, the idea that our societies are now relying on Facebook, YouTube, or Twitter to keep public records should give us pause for thought. While YouTube might contribute significant public value as an 'accidental' cultural archive, the question of whether YouTube should seriously take responsibility for preserving, archiving, and curating this archive as a public good is at least now being asked, even if it is far from being resolved.

# CHAPTER SIX

# YouTube's Competing Futures

## Who's Sorry Now?

There were two hybrid media events that brought Australia to the attention of the world in the months leading up to the writing of the first edition of this book in early 2008. One of them was apparently trivial, even stupid; the other was – or should have been – momentous. The differences in how they spread through YouTube and the broader media environment at the time help us think through the ongoing tensions between the 'two YouTubes', the broader formations of media culture that they represented, and what this meant for the future of digital media.

In January 2008, sixteen-year-old Melbourne teenager Corey Worthington made headlines for the mayhem caused when a party he hosted while his parents were out of town, and which he infamously advertised on MySpace and Facebook, got out of control (Hastie, 2008; Hughes, 2008). It made news in the mainstream media because it hit all the right targets – habitual moral anxiety around youth, connected to an equally habitual anxiety about the narcissism and exhibitionism associated with what were then called 'social networks', like MySpace and Facebook. The original *A Current Affair* segment on the story was (unofficially) uploaded to YouTube with the title 'Best Street Party Ever – Parents Yet to Find Out', and as at September 2017 it had been viewed 4.2 million times.[1]

Worthington's outrageously unrepentant on-camera behaviour (appearing naked from the waist up apart from a camouflage hoodie with a fur trim, a nipple piercing, and a pair of bright yellow sunglasses) when being interviewed for the segment landed him in hot water with the host, who attempted to play the parental or 'moral guardian' role, placing him in the counterpart role of the sheepishly guilty party. Worthington famously refused to play his role, displaying contempt for the idea that television current affairs (and, by extension, the mainstream media) had any more authority than the legions of YouTube users and MySpace members who, he appeared to knowingly predict, would take enormous mischievous delight in his continued defiance (Ramadge, 2008). And delight they did: mischief followed upon mischief, as clips of his famous refusal to remove his sunglasses and apologise on camera circulated with wild popularity on the web, and particularly on YouTube. Video parodies and visual memes proliferated in a matter of days; websites sardonically dedicated to the teenage 'party planner' appeared, often focusing on Corey's now-infamous yellow sunglasses or mashing up celebrity photographs with Corey-related slogans like 'It wasn't me.' Yet another website featured a game allowing visitors to slap some sense into the rogue teenager. Since Worthington's original MySpace page had been removed, and presumably in full knowledge the mainstream media would be looking forward to including it as part of their coverage of the event and ensuing uproar, Random Brainwave's 'John Surname' created a fake MySpace page, complete with a fabricated video masquerading as the original party invitation.[2] Adding insult to the news media's injury, those in the know about the prank were delighted when the UK's Channel 4 News aired the fake invitation video as part of their coverage of the scandal.[3] On YouTube, an amplification of the feedback loop between the event, its ongoing life in web culture, and the mainstream media was created as Fox News added the clips to their YouTube channel 'The Blast',[4] bringing the phenomenon to the attention of the wider US audience.

On the one hand, this event showed how out of step the

dominant media, especially commercial current affairs programs, were with the emergent vernaculars of Internet meme culture, with the layers of mischief, irony, and ambivalence that characterise the darker side of the popular web. On the other hand, it demonstrates the extent to which participants in social media had literacies far superior to those of mainstream media professionals in both the discourses (of youth, risk, and moral panic) and the format of current affairs; they were able to subvert and mobilise them using the rapid spreadability of their own mediated social networks and digital media platforms. The ethic behind all of this, however, was the very essence of trolling – or what Honoré de Balzac (1993 [1891]) described in his novel *The Bureaucrats* as 'mischief for mischief's sake'. Balzac describes the character of 'the egotist', who was 'famous for his practical jokes', was 'sharp, aggressive, and indiscreet, he did mischief for mischief's sake; above all, he attacked the weak, respected nothing and believed in nothing . . .'. (1993: 96). While highly anachronistic, this is an oddly apt description of Corey Worthington's media persona and the discourses employed by his swarm of 'supporters' – which resonates with the ethos of social media's 'toxic technocultures' (Massanari, 2017), including the trolling subcultures at that time associated with underground message-boards like 4Chan and now far more visible in mainstream social media culture (Phillips, 2015).

An entirely different kind of media event occurred on 13 February 2008. This was the day on which the Australian Prime Minister Kevin Rudd opened parliament with an official apology to Australia's Indigenous people, and the Stolen Generation in particular. It was an event that had been centuries in the making and was more than a decade overdue. It had been one of the hottest issues in Australian public life in previous elections and, other than the Federal election a few months earlier, it was arguably one of the most important, widely shared common experiences in the Australian cultural public sphere. In itself, the speech was not only an act of 'speaking', but also one of (at least performative) listening (Dreher, 2009). A meaningful official apology would not have been possible without an empathetic incorporation of the hundreds of stories of lives affected by the removal policies of previous governments; stories that had emerged over the previous decades and that were finally given the media space they deserved as the official event drew closer. When the day came, it was broadcast live from Parliament House on the television service of the Australian national broadcaster, the Australian Broadcasting Corporation (ABC). Ironically, on the eve of the official apology, the top YouTube search result for the combination of the keywords 'Australia' and 'sorry' was a clip from the original *A Current Affair* segment showing Corey Worthington's refusal to apologise for his behaviour.

Eventually the full ABC broadcast was uploaded to YouTube and by the end of the day had received a couple of hundred views. Slowly over the next 24 to 48 hours the Most Viewed pages of YouTube Australia began to fill with related videos. The kinds of videos that were uploaded (and with which audiences engaged) in response to the occasion collectively provide a fairly good summary of YouTube's diverse uses in general. They included straight uploads of the broadcast for the benefit of people who missed it or to record it for posterity; clips of the 'best bits' of the broadcast, providing the 'quotes' and 'catch-up' functions discussed in Chapter 3; a range of user-created videos using the audio of the speech and remixing it with users' own text-based commentaries and images in order to express individual perspectives and emotional reactions to the event; as well as the inevitable vlog entries offering personal perspectives and opinions on the apology. The text comments on these videos reflect the specific culture of political engagement in YouTube – they were generally characterised by very emotive, hyperbolic 'for-or-against' rhetoric, where raw racism was countered by equally raw moralising. More informed, nuanced, or deliberative perspectives struggled for space.

These two media events – both of which made a significant

impact within the culture of YouTube in symbiosis with the mainstream media – suggested two very different visions of participatory culture. Each of them represented a particular 'frequency of public writing' (Hartley, 2008a) – on the one hand, playful subversion with no purpose but exhibiting the awesome speed and creativity of 'viral' web culture; on the other, a cultural public sphere where conversations, self-mediated representation, and encounters with difference (which can be antagonistic and deaf to the other as much as they can be structured on mutual respect) can occur on popular terms, and yet with noticeably less dynamism and independence from official public culture than 'viral' culture exhibits. The Rudd speech had fewer than half a million views on YouTube as at October 2017; the video clip of *A Current Affair*'s segment on Corey's out-of-control party had more than 4 million.

In 2015, a reformed Corey Worthington was featured as a guest on the Australian morning TV talk show *Studio 10* in a segment entitled 'Corey Worthington Makes Good' – and, while more mature, he was still sporting his notorious yellow sunglasses.[5] But, while Worthington might have grown up, YouTube is still very much fertile ground for the forms of vernacular Internet culture characterised both by relatively benign trolling and systemic harassment and abuse; as before, generating interaction, drama, and media coverage. The difference is that, by 2017, that drama has become far more monetisable, not only by tabloid TV current affairs, but also by YouTube and the protagonists themselves, and the microcelebrity that comes with it is not always so 'micro' or ephemeral.

To take one illustrative news story from 2017, twenty-year-old Jake Paul began his career as a pre-teen Vine and YouTube star who eventually ended up landing a deal with Disney for a zany, MTV-style faux-reality show called *Bizaardvark* in which Paul plays a version of himself – a star of the online videoshar-ing network Vuuugle living in a share house with his crew and getting up to (mild) trouble. But in real life, Paul went too far with his ersatz bad-boy image and allowed his wild house party to get out of control, trashing the neighbourhood, losing the Disney deal (Bradley, 2017), and leading *The New York Times*'s Jonah Bromwich to dub him 'A Reality Villain for the YouTube Generation' (Bromwich, 2017). Jake Paul, of course, appeared utterly unconcerned. He has his own Multi-Channel Network, Team 10, with no pretensions to artistic achievement and no concern about the careful balance of authenticity and community: attention for attention's sake is his business model. The rap video he released to trash-talk his equally infamous brother Logan ('It's Everyday Bro') quickly became one of the most disliked YouTube videos of all time,[6] which will likely not harm his stated aim to "beat the Kardashians" in terms of social media followers.

At the time of writing, of course, he still hadn't apologised for the party. But maybe, if we write a third edition of this book, his infamy will be as obscure and faded as Worthington's, which has left only a *Know Your Meme* entry – and some archived YouTube clips – in its place.[7]

## Productive Tensions, Ongoing Challenges

YouTube launched without knowing exactly what it was going to be for, beyond large numbers of people sharing and consuming large amounts of video content. It is this relative under-determination that has created tensions between different uses of the platform, but that also explains the scale and diversity of its uses more than a decade later, and the innovations in genre, form, and audience engagement to which it has played host. In its early years, YouTube was large, loosely managed, and diverse, creating the conditions for 'interpretative flexibility' (Burgess, 2015) in terms of content, culture, and community. At the same time, this 'interpretative flexibility' fed into the company's restless search for a viable monetisation strategy, always precariously teetering between deals with television companies and music labels on the one side, and maintaining a core invitation to amateur content creators on the other. Like many other platforms, while under pressure around copyright and later around social behaviour and hate speech, it sought to maintain the impression that it was a neutral carrier, practising light-touch governance – just enough to stay on the right side of the letter of the law, but not enough to inhibit growth or generate fatal levels of dissatisfaction in the user community. In this early period, the platform was successful precisely because it did not seem to be targeting one particular use or market; and unlike some of the other video-sharing sites, YouTube didn't appear to be pursuing large media producers to the exclusion of amateur content creation. This openness, scale, and diversity are responsible for YouTube's success in the online video market, but they are also responsible for the ongoing and escalating conflicts around the platform's meanings, uses, and possible futures.

One of the biggest issues for YouTube's future has always been sustainable, profitable growth – given bandwidth costs, a crowded online video market, and the standing invitation (which remained as at October 2017) to 'anyone' to upload video to the platform. A core challenge will be to find a balance between mass popularisation (which YouTube has achieved), innovation, and sustainability (which requires long-term investment and a stable, loyal, and socially functioning community of both creators and audiences). Further, the new economics of value co-creation have brought with them new relationships of power and responsibility between users and platform providers, which platforms unevenly cultivate and protect, and which are increasingly subject to regulatory and governance challenges. YouTube, like all enterprises that rely on user co-creation, has needed to constantly find new ways to maintain its scale and rate of growth, adapting to the changing competitive and technological environment, while supporting cultural and aesthetic diversity, respecting the agency of the communities of users who work to help produce its various forms of value, and playing defence against the pressures of state-based regulation.

YouTube's competitive environment has also changed significantly over the course of its career as a platform, and the online video business had become far more complex and differentiated by 2017 than it was when YouTube was first launched. Smart televisions and streaming platforms like Netflix, Hulu, Amazon, and their equivalents in non-US markets have seen the advent of new forms of and ways of consuming television and other long-form premium content. Hulu pioneered premium television screening, followed by Netflix, Amazon, and analogous platforms in various international markets, which are not only in the streaming business but also in the original programming business. Vine exploded into popularity with a specific format of short, looping videos, launching the careers of many contemporary social media entertainers, who also operate seamlessly across various other platforms, including Instagram, Snapchat, Twitter, Facebook, Twitch, and WeChat.

YouTube has recently moved into the premium, subscription model of content with YouTube TV (a subscription-based service with DVR functionality offered in partnership with the major TV studios), which was launched in five US cities in May 2017 and was expanding to eight more US cities as at September 2017 (Popper, 2017; Deahl, 2017). Over various iterations of the subscription model including movie rentals and YouTube Red, the company has also ventured into original programming; but in doing so it has increasingly incorporated its formerly amateur star YouTubers (including Lilly Singh, Smosh, GigiGorgeous, and PewDiePie) as drawcard content channels; investing heavily in talent the company cannot fully own or control, and whose personal brands rely on authenticity and, in some cases, 'edginess' and non-conformity.

As it has formalised its commercial and governance structures, YouTube has responded to increased pressure to 'manage' the community and institute social norms more palatable to the public and the advertisers. For Kylie Jarrett (2008), this was what produced a fundamental corporate conflict between the original slogan 'Broadcast Yourself' and the trademark symbol that was once attached to it. While the company appeared to recognise that 'the anarchic, self-organising systems that have historically constituted YouTube are a fundamental and financially significant component of the site-as-experience and the site-as-business', and that therefore, 'to damage the community is to damage the company', 'the sustainability of this laissez faire position, and consequently the future of YouTube, is under threat by the very success these mechanisms have produced' (Jarrett, 2008: 137). The reality of this threat is illustrated by YouTube's history of selective monetisation and its impact on the platform's attention economy, beginning with reports that, once the Viacom lawsuit commenced, Google restricted ad sales to videos 'that have been posted or approved by media companies and other partners' (Delaney, 2008) – as little as 4 per cent of uploaders. Even before this, however, YouTube had to contend with a generally conservative advertising industry, which has complained about the lack of content guaranteed to be inoffensive enough for them to run advertising against (Delaney, 2008).

Throughout YouTube's career as a platform, there have been further, deepening convergences between 'community' and 'professional, corporate' logics, as the previous chapters have shown; but the tensions between the two YouTubes have not gone away. Content creators have always been subject to YouTube's Community Guidelines,[8] which cover nudity, hate speech, threats, and other misuses of the platform, such as consumer scams. Additionally, the platform has codified 'advertiser-friendly' content guidelines which it uses to maintain a 'safe' environment for advertisers, and with which content creators who wish to share advertising revenue must comply.[9] While the primary stated intent of these provisions is to guard against violent and extremist content (Gesenhues,

2017), there have been a number of controversies around the application of these guidelines to 'conservative' and far-right vloggers, who have built large followings on the platform. The platform's (increasingly automated) methods of operationalising these guidelines have generated intense controversies, particularly in the year-long series of events in 2017 known as the 'adpocalypse', which highlights the ongoing and problematic convergence between content regulation, values-based community governance, and the sociotechnical management of advertising.

In March 2017, after the *Guardian* realised its programmatic advertising was being placed against violent and extremist content on YouTube (Martinson, 2017), both they and a cascade of prominent UK and US brands pulled, or threatened to pull, their ads from the service. In April, YouTube announced that a threshold of 10,000 lifetime views per channel, plus a manual approval process, would be required in order to 'monetise' videos on a channel. The announcement read:

> Starting today, we will no longer serve ads on YPP videos until the channel reaches 10k lifetime views. This new threshold gives us enough information to determine the validity of a channel. It also allows us to confirm if a channel is following our community guidelines and advertiser policies. By keeping the threshold to 10k views, we also ensure that there will be minimal impact on our aspiring creators. And, of course, any revenue earned on channels with under 10k views up until today will not be impacted.
>
> In a few weeks, we'll also be adding a review process for new creators who apply to be in the YouTube Partner Program. After a creator hits 10k lifetime views on their channel, we'll review their activity against our policies. If everything looks good, we'll bring this channel into YPP and begin serving ads against their content. Together these new thresholds will help ensure revenue only flows to creators who are playing by the rules. (YouTube Creator Blog, 2017)

And in June, YouTube introduced a high-powered new combination of automated, manual, and consultative methods for

the identification of extremist content (Gesenhues, 2017), in
service of 'brand safety' (Marvin, 2017).

The strategy was imperfectly executed and caused significant upheaval in the YouTube community. YouTubers
reported finding their videos 'demonetised' overnight – that
is, they were automatically withdrawn from the revenue-
sharing arrangements that are part of the Partner Program.
The demonetisation of videos directly damaged YouTubers'
revenue streams, with some reporting losses of up to 80 per
cent of their income (Seavers, 2017). The additional overhead
required to apply to YouTube to have the ban on monetisation
lifted, as well as to wait for the result of an appeal or manual
review process, added significantly to the creators' already
high investments of time and energy.

While a significant amount of protest came from conservative and right-wing videobloggers associated with precisely the
kind of extremist content YouTube was trying to extract from
any association with brands, in *The Daily Dot*, Kris Seavers
(2017) reported on the more benign example of the Great
War channel,[10] which posts multiple educational videos about
the First World War each week and has more than 725,000
subscribers as at October 2017. Because of the potentially violent subject matter, Seavers reported, 75 of their videos were
automatically flagged for review. Like other content creators
in this position, Producer Florian Wittig turned to the Patreon
subscription service[11] as an alternative to revenue he might
otherwise generate through the YouTube Partner Program.
Patreon is more than a 'crowdfunding' platform – it allows
independent creators to run their own 'premium', subscription-based service, drawing revenue directly from loyal fans
in exchange for 'exclusive experiences and behind-the-scenes
content'. However, integrating Patreon with a YouTube channel requires outward links from the YouTube platform to
Patreon's, using the 'end-screen' feature. The catch is, the
'end-screen' feature as at 2017 could only link to YouTube-
approved sites (Grubb, 2017). In September 2017, YouTube

made changes that effectively meant that only members of the Partner Program could use these end-screen links, which in turn requires a manual review process and for the channel to pass the monetisation threshold of at least 10,000 subscribers, cutting small YouTube channels off from access to the Patreon platform (for discussion and links to YouTube's announcements of these changes, see Grubb, 2017). Patreon, too, has had to grapple with the challenges of content regulation and platform governance, amending its Community Guidelines to tighten the rules around hate speech and illegal content, and also to reduce the latitude it had formerly given to erotic content and sex workers – and, just like YouTube, causing outrage among creators who understand their livelihoods to be threatened by what is perceived to be arbitrary or purely self-interested governance moves by platforms (Cooper, 2017). Content creators' responses to the adpocalypse also demonstrate the fragility of YouTube's hold on its core talent, and the volatility of the operating environment for digital media intermediaries of all kinds.

The attempt to clean up YouTube's culture *for advertisers* problematically conflates sociocultural and political issues with commercial ones, and highlights the limits of the tensions between 'community' and 'corporate' logics – issues that have been notoriously problematic for Facebook and Twitter also. For now, the two YouTubes (the corporate media business and the open platform for vernacular culture) are still in dynamic tension – (Burgess, 2012a) – and as long as this tension remains in place then YouTube will continue to be a generative site of cultural innovation and diversity. However, the challenges around the social norms, transparency, and governance of YouTube are of extremely high societal significance – with material consequences for issues of trust, social cohesion, cultural diversity, and creative innovation. These challenges have been brought into sharp relief by the circulation on social media of disinformation and harmful content in 2016–17, highlighting the ongoing risks to the health of a media environment dominated by a small number of powerful platforms, and raising important questions about the role of platforms in ensuring that it is safe for women and minorities to participate in public culture and debate. It is important to think carefully about whether the quest for a remedy can be left entirely in the hands of the corporate platforms, which are understandably at least partly motivated by the desire to avoid regulatory burden and to help advertisers and corporate brands to feel 'safe' to associate with social media content and culture. Even if 'brand safety' (Marvin, 2017) does result in starving extreme and right-wing voices of funding, it may not work in service of diversity and inclusion. Advertiser-friendly content regulation – particularly using automated methods – can just as effectively smooth the edges off radical progressive politics or the witnessing of human rights abuses as it can work for the intended purpose of dampening abuse, hate speech, and extremist activity. And the conflation of sexual content and harmful speech in content regulation can often end up inadvertently discriminating against sexual and gender minorities – see Priddy (2017) for a discussion of how demonetisation has affected the visibility of LGBTQ videos, for example.

More than ever, there is a need for ongoing robust, rich, and situated research on YouTube, which must increasingly take into account the business environment, sociotechnical features, and governance mechanisms of the platform, as well as its cultural uses and its social norms. Throughout the book, we have pointed to the excellent work being done by scholars on a wide variety of topics for which YouTube proves to be a central object of analysis, and it appears that YouTube is a subject that is of ongoing and even increasing interest. Researchers have an important role to play in empirical studies and thick descriptions of digital media platforms, as well as thinking through the critical implications of the platform paradigm and its competing futures (Burgess, 2015). The roles of scholars include not only advocating for regulatory interventions where possible, but also showing how a situated and respectful understanding of user communities and their everyday practices can point the way to a more vibrant culture and improved governance. There is much more to do, and we look forward to being part of the project.

# Notes

## 1 How YouTube Matters

1 The full documents are available at: https://www.google.com/press/youtube_viacom_documents.html. For highlights, see Eaton, 2010.
2 A copy of the original YouTube pitch deck is available at: https://www.slideshare.net/AlexanderJarvis/youtube-pitch-deck
3 News Corporation, who had acquired MySpace the year before, were rumoured to be bidders (Allison and Waters, 2006).
4 According to a Nielsen news release, available at: www.nielsen-netratings.com/pr/pr_071106_2_UK.pdf
5 See https://www.alexa.com/siteinfo/youtube.com
6 This figure was obtained by running a wildcard search within YouTube, a method that ceased to work in April 2008.
7 This announcement was made as part of YouTube's eighth 'birthday' celebration video and reported widely, including at *The Verge*: https://www.theverge.com/2013/5/19/4345514/youtube-users-upload-100–hours-video-every-minute
8 Updated statistics from YouTube itself are available on its press page, which as at October 2017 was at: https://www.youtube.com/yt/about/press/
9 http://www.comscore.com/press/release.asp?press=2223
10 Karim himself told this story in a 2006 lecture at the University of Illinois at Urbana-Champaign, which was available on YouTube as at 2008, but has since been removed.
11 The 2005 press release is available at: http://www.marketwired.com/press-release/youtube-receives-35m-in-funding-from-sequoia-capital-736129.htm

## 2  YouTube and the Media

1 The official announcement of the launch of YouTube Kids is here: https://youtube.googleblog.com/2015/02/youtube-kids.html

2 http://www.thelonelyisland.com

3 The contest was hosted at http://youtube.com/mygrammymoment, but the URL is no longer live.

4 http://youtube.com/fromheretoawesome

5 See Crocker's 'Britney' video here: http://youtube.com/watch?v=kHmvkRoEowc

6 The 'Hey' clip is at http://youtube.com/watch?v=-_CS01gOd48

7 The video was spoofed in 2009 by filmmaker Kevin Smith as part of a promotion for his film *Clerks 2*. Introducing the spoof, Smith called on the clip as emblematic of YouTube. You can see Smith's spoof here: http://www.youtube.com/watch?v=zuuV7f3ux58 Smith is thanked in a note in the description to the original video, and a link to his spoof is included.

8 The 2014 Pixies video is at https://www.youtube.com/watch?v=fCRZrfonyZU

9 Heffernan's blog about television was available on the *New York Times* website at http://screens.blogs.nytimes.com/. In 2007, her coverage broadened from TV to Internet culture, and the blog morphed into http://themedium.blogs.nytimes.com, where her posts about Lonelygirl are still available. Heffernan moved over to Arts Beat, the *New York Times Magazine*'s blog about new arts and culture, in 2009, abandoning The Medium altogether.

10 According to the data presented in *PC Magazine*, YouTube's unique US Visitors jumped from 5,644,000 in March 2006 to 12,669,000 in May 2006, or an increase of around 124 per cent.

11 Accessible from within the US at http://www.hulu.com

12 Viacom's amended complaint can be found here: http://beckermanlegal.com/Documents/viacom_youtube_080418AmendedComplaint.pdf; YouTube's reply is available here: http://beckermanlegal.com/Documents/viacom_youtube_080523AnswertoAmendedComplaint.pdf

13 The press release is now off the web, but see the Mashable report on the filing of the suit: http://mashable.com/2007/03/13/viacom-youtube/

14 Socialblade's ranked lists of MCNs are available at: https://socialblade.com/youtube/top/networks

## 3 YouTube's Popular Culture

1 You can see early versions of the YouTube homepage at The Internet Archive's Wayback Machine (https://web.archive.org/web/*/http://youtube.com ), some of which have been captured as screenshots in articles (see Carrasco, 2013).

2 See Vidmeter.com's 2007 study of copyrighted videos on YouTube which reached a similar conclusion about the videos removed from the service: http://www.vidmeter.com/i/vidmeter_copyright_report.pdf

3 These removed videos were still coded where possible, based on available information and metadata.

4 In February 2008, the service was already testing technology to increase the visual and audio quality of video on the site. See http://cybernetnews.com/2008/02/29/watch-high-resolution-youtube-videos/

5 Thanks to Sam Ford for suggesting this term.

6 http://youtube.com/watch?v=LbkNxYaULBw

7 http://youtube.com/watch?v=GoLtUX_6IXY

8 The Streamy Awards are at https://www.streamys.org/

9 The video 'Youtube Poop – LEAVE MAMA LUIGI ALONE!' at http://youtube.com/watch?v=5kG43D1elWo uses clips from Chris Crocker's 'Leave Britney Alone' plea.

10 http://youtube.com/user/unsw

11 http://youtube.com/user/ucberkeleycampuslife

12 http://youtube.com/watch?v=czAaugp-S6I

13 http://youtube.com/user/fordmodels

14 https://www.youtube.com/user/redbull

15 http://youtube.com/user/nalts

16 http://www.youtube.com/user/charlestrippy

17 http://www.youtube.com/user/blunty3000

18 Mia Rose's channel is at http://youtube.com/user/miaarose

19 While the original resource has been replaced by much more elaborate 'Creator Academy' resources, the original promo video, which outlines the Playbook's content, is available at https://www.youtube.com/watch?v=nzdD6qnczDo

20 The NextUp program's official YouTube page is at http://www.youtube.com/creators

21 The official information about its YouTube Spaces is at https://www.youtube.com/yt/space/

22 YouTube's seventh birthday video is at https://www.youtube.com/watch?v=GLQDPHoulCg&feature=youtu.be

23 "The A-Z of YouTube" is at https://www.youtube.com/
watch?v=WwoKkq685Hk

24 The Tubefilter YouTube Millionaires column homepage is at:
http://www.tubefilter.com/category/youtube-millions/

25 As at May 2013 it was still possible to get at the most subscribed
videos by visiting http://youtube.com/charts; as at October 2017
this page redirects to the music charts.

26 The most popular channels list was at http://youtube.com/charts
as at May 2013, but as at October 2017 redirects to the YouTube
'Top 40' music charts.

27 See https://socialblade.com/youtube/

## 4 THE YOUTUBE COMMUNITY

1 12seconds.tv closed in 2010, and fantasticblabbings' longer
vlog entry on the topic (originally at http://www.youtube.com/
watch?v=BBxjscfmon4) is no longer available on YouTube.
However YouTuber Kenny Seidens published a montage-
style tribute video at https://www.youtube.com/watch?v=L_
WJDavStTc which gives a good sense of the range of ways
videobloggers participated in 12seconds.TV.

2 In one important improvement, YouTube was made available
in HTML5 by default on most browsers by 2015 (YouTube
Engineering and Developers Blog, 2015).

3 The introduction of automatic captions was announced at the
Google Blog: https://googleblog.blogspot.com.au/2009/11/
automatic-captions-in-youtube.html

4 The caption correction tool is at http://nomorecraptions.com

5 See TheDeafCaptioner on Medium: https://medium.com/@
mlockrey

6 'Mission Improbable: An Almost Shout-Out' was originally here:
http://youtube.com/watch?v=rV2tG9m_Pow, but is no longer
available.

7 Peter Oakley died of cancer in 2014. His last video was posted a
few months before his death.

8 Oakley's first video is available here: http://youtube.com/
watch?v=p_YMigZmUuk

9 Computing for the Terrified is here: http://youtube.com/
watch?v=jKJ8jRXNJJg

10 The 'Nalts on Oprah? Noprah', video is at http://youtube.com/
watch?v=c_ZNVES1wGw

11 Renetto's video was posted at http://youtube.com/
watch?v=IYRucYmDsM0 but is no longer available.
12 Paperlilies' 'RIP the Golden Age of YouTube' is at https://www.
youtube.com/watch?v=Jk05NZUqVZo
13 Blunty's channel is at https://www.youtube.com/user/
Blunty3000, and as at October 2017 had 333,200 subscribers.
14 Hanner's channel is still at https://www.youtube.com/user/
xgobobeanx and has 28,000 subscribers.
15 The YouTube Stars website was at http://www.bkserv.net/YTS/
YTMostViewed.aspx but no longer exists. The Internet Archive
Wayback Machine's last known version of this page redirected
to YouTube, indicating that the website was either acquired or
forced to close by YouTube.
16 The video has since been removed.
17 LisaNova's channel is at: https://www.youtube.com/user/
LisaNova and had 530,000 subscribers as at October 2017.

## 5 YouTube's Cultural Politics

1 The invitation to respond to the question 'what does YOUR
fridge say about YOU?' was here http://youtube.com/watch?v=
sqduQT242Iw, but is no longer available. The invitation was itself
a response to a humorous vlog by Asian-American YouTuber
kevjumba (whose channel was later renamed to 'kev', with 2.9m
subscribers as at October 2017) about Asian stereotypes.
2 The Creators for Change program (for 'creators who are tackling
social issues and promoting awareness, tolerance and empathy
on their YouTube channels') is detailed here: https://www.
youtube.com/yt/creators-for-change/
3 Account settings are at: https://www.youtube.com/account

## 6 YouTube's Competing Futures

1 The *A Current Affair* segment is at: https://youtu.be/
xcoCB6URrVo
2 Random Brainwave discussed the hoax here: http://
randombrainwave.blogspot.com/2008/01/world-gets-brainwavd.
html – this blog is no longer available.
3 Channel 4's story was at http://youtube.com/watch?v=sQgg7SIW
ppo, but is no longer available.

4 Fox's 'The Blast' episode featuring the story was available
as an unofficial upload here: http://youtube.com/
watch?v=Hnls6FocNy4, but is no longer available.
5 The *Studio 10* segment on the reformed Worthington is here:
https://www.youtube.com/watch?v=Gl9l51wacgo
6 Paul's video was at no. 7 on the most-disliked playlist as at 3
October 2017: https://www.youtube.com/playlist?list=PLirAqAtl_
h20iismidr5SbvB8Mf7Ve6Aa
7 The Know Your Meme entry 'Corey Worthington's Party' is at
http://knowyourmeme.com/memes/events/corey-worthingtons-
party
8 The YouTube Community Guidelines are at https://www.
youtube.com/yt/policyandsafety/communityguidelines.html
9 YouTube's advertiser-friendly content guidelines are explained at
https://support.google.com/youtube/answer/6162278?hl=en
10 The Great War channel is at https://www.youtube.com/user/
TheGreatWar
11 See https://www.patreon.com/

# References

'Best YouTube Videos' (2007) *A Current Affair*. Nine Network, Australia, 31 December.

'Premier League to take action against YouTube' (2007) *Telegraph Online*, 23 May. Available at: http://www.telegraph.co.uk/sport/foot ball/2312532/Premier-League-to-take-action-against-YouTube.html

'Teachers in Website Closure Call' (2007) *BBC.co.uk*, 1 August. Available at: http://news.bbc.co.uk/2/hi/uk_news/scotland/6925444.stm

'UPDATE 2-Mediaset sues Google, YouTube; seeks $780 mln' (2008) Reuters-UK, 30 July: Available at: http://uk.reuters.com/article/governmentFilingsNews/idUKL04549520080730

'Your 15 Minutes of Fame...Um, Make that 10 Minutes or Less' (2006) *Broadcasting Ourselves; The Official YouTube Blog* 26 March http://youtube-global.blogspot.com/2006/03/your-15-minutes-of-fameummmmmake-that-10.html

'YouTube's Most Watched' (2007) *Today Tonight*. Seven Network, Australia, 31 December.

'YouTube's Greatest Hits With The Billionaire Founders' (2007) *The Oprah Winfrey Show*. Available at: http://www.oprah.com/tows/pastshows/200711/tows_past_20071106.jhtml

'YouTube Tackles Bullying Online' (2007) *BBC.co.uk*, 19 November. Available at: http://news.bbc.co.uk/1/hi/education/7098978.stm

Abidin, Crystal (2015a) 'Micromicrocelebrity: Branding Babies on the Internet'. *M/C Journal* 18(5): http://www.journal.media-culture.org.au/index.php/mcjournal/article/view/1022

— (2015b) 'Communicative intimacies: Influencers and Perceived Interconnectedness'. *Ada: A Journal of Gender, New Media, and Technology* 8: http://adanewmedia.org/2015/11/issue8-abidin/

Adegoke, Yinka (2006) 'PluggedIn: New rock stars use Web videos to win fans'. *Reuters News*, 25 August. Accessed via Factiva database.

Allison, Kevin and Richard Waters (2006) 'Google and Murdoch Among the Suitors Circling YouTube'. *Financial Times*, London, 7 October. Accessed via Factiva database.

Anderson, Monica (2015) '5 Facts About Online Video, for YouTube's tenth Birthday'. *FactTank: News in the Numbers.* Pew Research Centre, 12 February. Available at: http://www.pewresearch.org/fact-tank/2015/02/12/5-facts-about-online-video-for-youtubes-10th-birthday/

Andrejevic, Mark (2003) *Reality TV: The Work of Being Watched.* Lanham, MD: Rowman and Littlefield.

—(2013) 'Estranged Free Labor'. *Digital Labor: The Internet as Playground and Factory.* Ed. Trebor Scholz. New York and London: Routledge, pp. 149–64.

Arrington, Michael (2005) 'Comparing the Flickrs of Video'. *TechCrunch,* 6 November. Available at: http://www.techcrunch.com/2005/11/06/the-flickrs-of-video/

Arthur, Charles (2006) 'Has YouTube changed since its purchase this month by Google?' *Guardian,* London, 26 October. Accessed via Factiva database.

Aufderheide, Patricia and Peter Jaszi (2011) *Reclaiming Fair Use: How to Put Balance Back in Copyright.* Chicago: University of Chicago Press.

Balzac, Honoré de (1993 [1891]) *The Bureaucrats.* Ed. Marco Diani, Trans. Charles Foulkes. Evanston: Northwestern University Press.

Baker, Sarah Louise (2004) 'Pop in(to) the Bedroom: Popular Music in Pre-Teen Girls' Bedroom Culture'. *European Journal of Cultural Studies* 7(1): 75–93.

Bakioğlu, Burcu S. (2016) 'Exposing Convergence: YouTube, Fan Labour, and Anxiety of Cultural Production in *Lonelygirl15*'. *Convergence: The International Journal of Research into New Media Technologies*: 1–21. Online first DOI: https://doi.org/10.1177/135485 6516655527

Banet-Weiser, Sarah (2012) *Authentic™: The politics of Ambivalence in a Brand Culture.* New York: New York University Press.

Banks, John and Sal Humphreys (2008) 'The Labour of User Co-Creators: Emergent Social Network Markets?' *Convergence: The International Journal of Research into New Media Technologies* 14(4): 401–18.

Bawden, Tom and Dan Sabbagh (2006) 'Google to buy YouTube for $1.65bn'. *The Times,* London, 10 October, p. 53.

Becker, Anne (2007) 'YouTube to Viacom: We Will Pull Your Clips'. *Broadcasting and Cable,* 2 February.

Becker, Howard S. (1982) *Art Worlds.* Berkeley: University of California Press.

Benkler, Yochai (2006) *The Wealth of Networks: How Social Production Transforms Markets and Freedom.* New Haven and London: Yale University Press.

Berry, Trine Bjørkman (2015) *The Film of Tomorrow: A Cultural History of Videoblogging.* Doctoral Dissertation. University of Sussex. Available at: http:// sro.sussex.ac.uk/53713/

Berryman, Rachel and Misha Kavka (2017) '"I Guess a Lot of People See Me as a Big Sister or a Friend": The Role of Intimacy in the Celebrification of Beauty Vloggers'. *Journal of Gender Studies* 26(3): 307–20.

Biggs, John (2006) 'A Video Clip Goes Viral, and a TV Network Wants to Control It'. *New York Times*, New York, 20 February. Available at: http://www.nytimes.com/

Blakely, Rhys (2007) 'YouTube fails to satisfy critics over copyright'. *The Times*, London. 17 October, p. 49.

Bovill, Moira and Sonia Livingstone (2001) 'Bedroom Culture and the Privatization of Media Use'. *Children and Their Changing Media Environment: A European Comparative Study.* Mahwah, NJ: Lawrence Earlbaum Associates, pp. 179–200.

boyd, danah (2007) 'Why Youth (Heart) Social Network Sites: The Role of Networked Publics in Teenage Social Life'. *MacArthur Foundation Series on Digital Learning – Youth, Identity, and Digital Media Volume.* Ed. David Buckingham. Cambridge, MA: MIT Press.

— (2017) 'Did Media Literacy Backfire?' *Journal of Applied Youth Studies* 1(4): 83–9.

boyd, danah m. and Nicole B. Ellison (2007) 'Social Network Sites: Definition, History, and Scholarship'. *Journal of Computer-Mediated Communication* 13(1): 210–30. Available at: http://jcmc.indiana.edu/vol13/issue1/boyd.ellison.html

Bradley, Laura (2017). 'Why Disney Just Severed Ties with a Famously Obnoxious YouTuber'. *Vanity Fair*, 25 July. Available at: https://www.vanityfair.com/hollywood/2017/07/jake-paul-disney-bizaard vark-neighbors-controversy

Broersma, Matthew (2007) 'Viacom to YouTube: Take Down Pirated Clips'. *ZDNet*, 2 February. Available at: http://news.zdnet.com/2100-9595-6155771.html

Bromwich, Jonah Engel (2017) 'Jake Paul, a Reality Villain for the YouTube Generation'. *The New York Times*, 20 July. Available at: https://www.nytimes.com/2017/07/20/arts/who-is-jake-paul.html

Brügger, Niels (2017) 'Web History and Social Media'. *The Sage Handbook of Social Media.* Eds Jean Burgess, Alice Marwick, and Thomas Poell. London: Sage, pp. 196–212.

Bruno, Antony (2007) 'The YouTube Conundrum', *Billboard*, 3 March. Accessed via Factiva database.

Bruns, Axel (2008) *Blogs, Wikipedia, Second Life, and Beyond: From Production to Produsage*. New York: Peter Lang.

Burgess, Jean (2006) 'Hearing Ordinary Voices: Cultural Studies, Vernacular Creativity and Digital Storytelling'. *Continuum: Journal of Media and Cultural Studies* 2(20): 201–14.

— (2008) '"All Your Chocolate Rain are Belong to Us?" Viral Video, YouTube and the dynamics of participatory culture'. In *Video Vortex Reader: Responses to YouTube*. Amsterdam: Institute of Network Cultures, pp. 101–9.

— (2012a) 'YouTube and the Formalisation of Amateur Media'. *Amateur Media: Social, Cultural and Legal Perspectives*. Eds Dan Hunter, Ramon Lobato, Megan Richardson, and Julian Thomas. New York, Oxford: Routledge, pp. 53–8.

— (2012b) 'The iPhone Moment, the Apple Brand and the Creative Consumer: From "Hackability and Usability" to Cultural Generativity'. *Studying Mobile Media: Cultural Technologies, Mobile Communication, and the iPhone*. Eds Larissa Hjorth, Ingrid Richardson, and Jean Burgess. New York and London: Routledge, pp. 28–42.

— (2015) 'From "Broadcast Yourself!" to "Follow your Interests": Making Over Social Media'. *International Journal of Cultural Studies* 18(3): 281–5.

— (2016) 'Digital Media and Generations'. *Communication Across the Life Span*. Ed. Jon F. Nussbaum. New York: Peter Lang, pp. 21–6.

— (2017) 'Convergence'. *Keywords for Media Studies*. Eds Laurie Ouellette and Jonathan Gray. New York: New York University Press, pp. 47–9.

Burgess, Jean and Joshua Green (2008) 'The Entrepreneurial Vlogger: Participatory Culture Beyond the Professional-Amateur Divide'. *The YouTube Reader*. Eds Pelle Snickars and Patrick Vonderau. Stockholm: National Library of Sweden/Wallflower Press, pp. 89–107.

Burgess, Jean and Ariadna Matamoros-Fernández (2016) 'Mapping Sociocultural Controversies Across Digital Media Platforms: One Week of #gamergate on Twitter, YouTube, and Tumblr'. *Communication Research and Practice* 2(1): 79–96.

Burgess, Jean, Peta Mitchell, and Felix Münch (2018) 'Social Media Rituals: The Uses of Celebrity Death in Digital Culture'. *A Networked Self; Birth, Life, Death*. Ed. Zizi Papacharissi. New York: Routledge (in press).

Butsch, Richard (2000) *The Making of American Audiences: From Stage to Television, 1750–1990*. Cambridge: Cambridge University Press.

Butterfield, Stewart (2006) 'Eyes of the World.' *FlickrBlog*. Available at http://blog.flickr.com/flickrblog/2006/03/eyes_of_the_wor.html

Byrne, Seamus (2005) 'Be seen, read, heard'. *The Sydney Morning Herald*, Sydney, 3 September, p. 4.

Callon, Michel (1998) 'Introduction: The Embeddedness of Economic Markets in Economics'. *The Laws of the Markets*. Ed. Michel Callon. Oxford: Blackwell, pp. 1–57.

Campbell, Angela J. (2016) 'Rethinking Children's Advertising Policies for the Digital Age'. 29 Loy. Consumer L. Rev. 1. Available at SSRN: https://ssrn.com/abstract=2911892

Carrasco, Ed (2013)'YouTube Grows Up: A Visual History of How the Video-Sharing Site Has Changed Over the Past 8 Years'. *New Media Rockstars* 14 February. Available at: http://newmediarockstars.com/2013/02/youtube-grows-up-a-visual-history-of-how-the-video-sharing-site-has-changed-over-the-past-8-years/

Cha, Meeyoung, Haewoon Kwak, Pablo Rodriguez, Yong-Yeol Ahn, and Sue Moon (2007) 'I Tube, You Tube, Everybody Tubes: Analyzing the World's Largest User Generated Content Video System'. Paper presented at *IMC'07: Internet Measurement Conference*, San Diego, CA.

Charny, Ben (2007) 'YouTube Gave User's Data to Paramount's Lawyers'. *Dow Jones News Service*, 21 October. Accessed via Factiva database.

Chonin, Neva (2006) 'Who's That Girl?' *San Francisco Chronicle*, 3 September, p. 14.

Cohen, Stanley (1972) *Folk Devils and Moral Panics: The Creation of the Mods and Rockers*. London: MacGibbon and Kee.

Cooper, Daniel (2017) 'The real consequences of Patreon's adult content crackdown'. *Engadget*, 27 October. Available at: https://www.engadget.com/2017/10/27/patreon-adult-content-crowdfunding-uncertainty/

Couldry, Nick (2000) *The Place of Media Power: Pilgrims and Witnesses of the Media Age*. London and New York: Routledge.

— (2003) *Media Rituals: A Critical Approach*. London and New York: Routledge.

— (2006) *Listening Beyond the Echoes: Media, Ethics and Agency in an Uncertain World*. Boulder, CO: Paradigm.

Couldry, Nick and Tim Markham (2007) 'Celebrity Culture and Public Connection: Bridge Or Chasm?' *International Journal of Cultural Studies* 10(4): 403–21.

Craig, David and Stuart Cunningham (2017) 'Toy Unboxing: Living in a (n Unregulated) Material World. *Media International Australia*

online first: http://journals.sagepub.com/doi/abs/10.1177/1329878
X17693700

Cunningham, Stuart and David Craig (2017) 'Being "really real" on YouTube: Authenticity, Community and Brand Culture in Social Media Entertainment'. *Media International Australia* 164(1): 71–81.

Cunningham, Stuart, David Craig, and Jon Silver (2016) 'YouTube, Multichannel Networks and the Accelerated Evolution of the New Screen Ecology'. *Convergence: The International Journal of Research into New Media Technologies* 22(4): 376–91.

Cunningham, Stuart and Tina Nguyen (2000) 'Popular Media of the Vietnamese Diaspora'. *Floating Lives: The Media and Asian Diasporas*. Eds Stuart Cunningham and John Sinclair. St Lucia, Queensland: University of Queensland Press, pp. 91–135.

Davis, Joshua (2006) 'The Secret World of Lonelygirl'. *Wired* 14(12): 232–9.

Deahl, Dani (2017) 'YouTube TV is Expanding to Eight More Cities'. *The Verge*, 14 September. Available at: https://www.theverge.com/tech/2017/9/14/16308664/youtube-tv-google-eight-more-cities

Delaney, Kevin J. (2006) 'Garage Brand: With NBC Pact, YouTube Site Tries to Build a Lasting Business'. *The Wall Street Journal*, 27 June, p. A1.

Delaney, Kevin J. (2008) 'Google Push To Sell Ads On YouTube Hits Snags – Video Site Is Key To Diversification; The Lawsuit Factor'. *Wall Street Journal*, New York, 9 July, p. A.1.

Deuze, Mark (2007) *Media Work*. Cambridge: Polity.

Diana, Alison (2011) 'YouTube Acquires Next New Networks'. *Information Week*, 8 March.

Dreher, Tanja (2009) 'Listening Across Difference: Media and Multiculturalism Beyond the Politics of Voice'. *Continuum* 23(4): 445–458.

Driscoll, Catherine and Melissa Gregg (2008) 'Broadcast Yourself: Moral Panic, Youth Culture and Internet Studies'. *Youth, Media and Culture in the Asia Pacific Region*. Eds Usha M. Rodrigues and Belinda Smaill. Newcastle: Cambridge Scholars Publishing, pp. 71–86.

Drotner, Kirsten (1999) 'Dangerous Media? Panic Discourses and Dilemmas of Modernity'. *Paedagogica Historica* 35(3): 593–619.

— (2000) 'Difference and Diversity: Trends in Young Danes' Media Uses'. *Media, Culture and Society* 22(2): 149–66.

— (2008) 'Leisure is Hard Work: Digital Practices and Future Competencies'. *Youth, Identity, and Digital Media*. Ed. David Buckingham. The John D. And Catherine T. Macarthur Foundation

Series on Digital Media and Learning. Cambridge, MA: The MIT Press, pp. 167–84.

Duffy, Brooke E. (2017) *(Not) Getting Paid to Do What You Love: Gender, Social Media, and Aspirational Work*. New Haven: Yale University Press.

Dupere, Katie (2016) 'Deaf YouTubers Lead Movementto Put an End to Crappy Video Captions'. *Mashable*, 11 November. Available at https://mashable.com/2016/11/11/youtube-closed=captioning-nomorecraptions/

Eaton, Kit (2010) '"Steal It" and Other Internal YouTube Emails from Viacom's Copyright Suit'. *Fast Company*, 18 March. Available at: https://www.fastcompany.com/1588353/steal-it-and-other-internal-youtube-emails-viacoms-copyright-suit

Edwards, Scott (2017) 'When YouTube Removes Violent Videos, It Impedes Justice'. *Wired*, 10 July. Available at: https://www.wired.com/story/when-youtube-removes-violent-videos-it-impedes-justice/

Elfman, Doug (2006) 'Wag of the Finger at YouTube'. *The Chicago Sun-Times*, Chicago, 31 October. Accessed via Factiva database.

Elias, Paul (2006) 'Google Reportedly Talking With YouTube'. *Associated Press Newswires*, 7 October. Accessed via Factiva database.

Ellcessor, Elizabeth (2016) *Restricted Access: Media, Disability, and the Politics of Participation*. New York: New York University Press.

Ellis, Katie (2010) 'A Purposeful Rebuilding: YouTube, Representation, Accessibility and the Socio-Political Space of Disability'. *Telecommunications Journal of Australia* 60(2): 1–12.

Fine, Jon (2006) 'The Strange Case of lonelygirl15'. *Business Week*, 11 September, p. 22.

Fiske, John (1989) *Reading the Popular*. Boston: Unwin Hyman.

— (1992a) *Understanding Popular Culture*, London and New York: Routledge.

— (1992b) 'The Cultural Economy of Fandom'. *The Adoring Audience: Fan Culture and Popular Media*. Ed. Lisa A. Lewis. London: Routledge, pp. 30–49.

Flaxman, Seth, Sharad Goel, and Justin M. Rao (2016) 'Filter Bubbles, Echo Chambers, and Online News Consumption'. *Public Opinion Quarterly* 80(S1): 298–320.

Gal, Noam, Limor Shifman, and Zohar Kampf (2016) '"It Gets Better": Internet memes and the construction of collective identity'. *New Media and Society* 18(8): 1698–1714.

Galloway, Anne, Jonah Brucker-Cohen, Lalya Gaye, and Elizabeth

Goodman (2004) 'Panel: Design for Hackability'. *Designing Interactive Systems (DIS2004)*. Available at: http://www.sigchi.org/DIS2004/Documents/Panels/DIS2004_Design_for_Hackability.pdf

Galperin, Eva (2011) '2011 in Review: Nymwars'. *Electronic Frontier Foundation*, 26 December. Available at: https://www.eff.org/deep links/2011/12/2011-review-nymwars

Gandy, Oscar H. (2002) 'The Real Digital Divide: Citizens Versus Consumers'. *Handbook of New Media: Social Shaping and Consequences of ICTs*. Eds Leah A. Lievrouw and Sonia Livingstone. London: Sage, pp. 448–60.

Gannes, Liz. (2006) 'Jawed Karim: How YouTube Took Off'. *Gigacom*, 26 October. Available at: http://gigaom.com/2006/10/26/jawed-karim-how-youtube-took-off/

Gehl, Robert (2009) 'YouTube *As* Archive: Who Will Curate this Digital *Wunderkammer?*' *International Journal of Cultural Studies* 12(1): 43–160.

Geist, Michael (2006) 'Why YouTube Won't Become Napster Redux'. *The Toronto Star*, Toronto, 16 October, p. C3.

Gell, Alfred (1998) *Art and Agency: An Anthropological Theory*. Oxford: Oxford University Press.

Gentile, G. (2006) 'Online Mystery of Video-Diary Posting by "Lonelygirl15" Continues to Deepen'. *Associated Press Newswires*, 11 September. Accessed via Factiva database.

Gesenhues, Amy (2017) 'YouTube: We've Manually Reviewed 1M+ videos to Improve Brand Safety Processes'. *Marketing Land*, 19 October. Available at: https://marketingland.com/youtube-man ually-reviewed-1m-videos-improve-brand-safety-efforts-around-extre mist-content-226579

Gibbs, Martin, James Meese, Michael Arnold, Bjorn Nansen, and Marcus Carter (2015) '#Funeral and Instagram: Death, Social Media, and Platform Vernacular'. *Information, Communication and Society* 18(3): 255–268.

Gibson, Margaret (2015) 'YouTube and Bereavement Vlogging: Emotional Exchange Between Strangers'. *Journal of Sociology* 52(4): 631–45.

Gill, Phillipa, Martin Arlitt, Li Zongpeng, and Anirban Mahanti (2007) 'YouTube Traffic Characterization: A View From the Edge'. Paper presented at *IMC'07*, San Diego, CA.

Gillespie, Tarleton (2010) 'The Politics of "Platforms"'. *New Media and Society* 12(3), 347–364.

— (2016) 'Algorithms'. *Digital Keywords: A Vocabulary of Information*

*Society and Culture.* Ed. Benjamin Peters. Princeton and Oxford: Princeton University Press, pp. 18–30.

— (2017) 'Governance Of and By Platforms'. *The Sage Handbook of Social Media.* Eds Jean Burgess, Alice Marwick, and Thomas Poell. London: Sage, forthcoming. Preprint: http://culturedigitally. org/wp-content/uploads/2016/06/Gillespie-Governance-ofby-Platforms-PREPRINT.pdf

Goetz, Thomas (2005) 'Reinventing Television'. *Wired* 13(9). Available at: http://www.wired.com/wired/archive/13.09/stewart.html

Goo, Sara Kehaulani (2006) 'Ready for its Close-Up; With Google Said to be a Suitor, YouTube Enters Mainstream'. *The Washington Post,* 7 October, p. D1.

Gorali, Nir (2014) 'Israeli YouTube Stars No Longer Mime the Pixies, They Direct the Band's Video'. *Haaretz,* 16 September. Available at: https://www.haaretz.com/israel-news/culture/theater/.premi um-1.616075

Gracy, Karen F. (2007) 'Moving Image Preservation and Cultural Capital'. *Library Trends* 56(1): 183–98.

Graham, Jefferson (2005) 'Video websites pop up, invite postings; Digital cameras spread capability'. *USA Today,* National, 22 November, p. B3.

Gray, Jonathan, Cornel Sandvoss, and C. Lee Harrington (2008) 'Introduction: Why Study Fans?' *Fandom: Identities and Communities in a Media World.* Eds Jonathan Gray, Cornell Sandvoss, and C. Lee Harrington. New York and London: New York University Press, pp. 1–16.

Green, Joshua (2008) 'Why Do They Call it TV When It's Not On the Box? "New" Television Services and "Old" Television Functions'. *Media International Australia Incorporating Culture and Policy* 126 (February): 95–105.

Green, Joshua and Henry Jenkins (2009) 'The Moral Economy of Web 2.0: Audience Research and Convergence Culture'. *Media Industries: History, Theory and Methods.* Eds Jennifer Holt and Alisa Perren. Chichester/Oxford: Wiley.

Grossman, Lev (2006a) 'How to Get Famous in 30 Seconds'. *TIME.* Available at http://time.com/time/magazine/article/0,9171,1184 060,00.html

— (2006b) 'Time's Person of the Year: You'. *TIME.* Available at: http://time.com/time/magazine/article/0,9171,1569514,00.html

Grubb, Jeff (2017) 'YouTube Creates Confusion by Herding Creators into Partner Program to Fight "Abuse"'. *VentureBeat,* 28 September. Available at: https://venturebeat.com/2017/09/28/youtube-patre

on-endscreen-links/

Gutelle, Sam (2016) 'There Are Now 2,000 YouTube Channels With at Least One Million Subscribers'. *TubeFilter*, 4 April. Available at: http://www.tubefilter.com/2016/04/04/youtube-millionaires-2000-channels/

Hall, Stuart (1981) 'Notes on Deconstructing "the Popular"'. *People's History and Socialist Theory*. Ed. Raphael Samuel. London: Routledge and Kegan Paul, pp. 227–39.

Hall, Stuart et al. (1978) *Policing the Crisis: Mugging, the State, and Law and Order*. London: Macmillan.

Harley, D. and G. Fitzpatrick (2008) 'YouTube and Intergenerational Communication: The Case of Geriatric1927'. *Universal Access in the Information Society*.

Harris, John (2006) 'The Vision Thing'. *Guardian*, London, 11 October, p. 6.

Hartley, John (1999) *Uses of Television*. London: Routledge.

— (2004) 'The "Value Chain of Meaning" and the New Economy'. *International Journal of Cultural Studies* 1(7): 129–41.

— (2008a) *Television Truths: Forms of Knowledge in Popular Culture*. London: Blackwell.

— (2008b) '"Numbers Over Knowledge"? Journalism and Popular Culture'. *Handbook of Journalism Studies*. Eds Karin Wahl-Jorgensen and Thomas Hanitzsch. Mahwah, NJ: Lawrence Erlbaum Associates, forthcoming 2009. Author version cited.

Hartley, John, Jean Burgess, and Joshua Green (2007) '"Laughs and Legends", or the Furniture That Glows? Television as History'. *Australian Cultural History* 26: 15–36.

Hastie, David (2008), 'Web Invite Sees Party Explode into Drunken Rampage'. *The Courier Mail*, Brisbane, 14 January. Accessed via Factiva Database.

Heath, Stephen (1990) 'Representing Television'. *Logics of Television: Essays in Cultural Criticism*. Ed. Patricia Mellencamp. London: BFI and Indiana: Indiana University Press, pp. 267–302.

Hebdige, D. (1988) *Hiding in the Light: On Images and Things*. London: Routledge.

Heffernan, Virginia and Tom Zeller Jr. (2006) 'Well, It Turns Out That Lonelygirl Really Wasn't'. *The New York Times*, New York, 13 September. Accessed via Factiva database.

Helmond, Anne (2015). 'The Platformization of the Web: Making Web Data Platform Ready'. *Social Media + Society*. Online first DOI: 10.1177/2056305115603080

Hermes, Joke (2005) *Re-Reading Popular Culture*. Malden: Blackwell.

— (2006) 'Hidden Debates: Rethinking the Relationship Between Popular Culture and the Public Sphere'. *Javnost – The Public* 13(4): 27–44.

Herring, Susan C. (2008) 'Questioning the Generational Divide: Technological Exoticism and Adult Constructions of Online Youth Identity'. *Youth, Identity, and Digital Media*. Ed. David Buckingham. The John D. and Catherine T. Macarthur Foundation Series on Digital Media and Learning. Cambridge, MA: The MIT Press, pp. 71–92.

Hilderbrand, Lucas (2007) 'YouTube: Where Cultural Memory and Copyright Converge'. *Film Quarterly* 61(1): 48–57.

Hobbs, Renée (1998) 'The Seven Great Debates in the Media Literacy Movement'. *Journal of Communication* 48(1): 6–32.

Hof, Karina (2006) 'Something You Can Actually Pick Up: Scrapbooking as a Form and Forum of Cultural Citizenship'. *European Journal of Cultural Studies* 3(9): 363–84.

Hoggart, Richard (1957) *The Uses of Literacy*. Harmondsworth: Penguin.

Hughes, Gary (2008) '500 Teens Rampage as Police End Party'. *The Australian*, 14 January. Accessed via Factiva database.

Humphreys, Sal (2005) 'Productive Players: Online Computer Games' Challenge to Conventional Media Forms'. *Journal of Communication and Critical/Cultural Studies* 1(2): 36–50.

Hutchinson, Bill (2007) 'YouTube Hails Web Wonders', *New York Daily News*, 27 March. Accessed via Factiva database.

Jarrett, Kylie (2008) 'Beyond Broadcast Yourself™: The Future of YouTube'. *Media International Australia* 126: 132–44.

Jenkins, Henry (2006a) *Convergence Culture: Where Old and New Media Collide*. New York: New York University Press.

— (2006b) *Fans, Bloggers and Gamers: Exploring Participatory Culture*. New York: New York University Press.

— (2006c) 'YouTube and the Vaudeville Aesthetic'. *Confessions of an Aca-Fan*. 20 November. Available at: http://www.henryjenkins.org/2006/11/youtube_and_the_vaudeville_aes.html

— (2009) 'What Happened Before YouTube.' *YouTube: Online Video & Participatory Culture*. Jean Burgess and Joshua Green. Cambridge: Polity, pp. 109–125.

Jenkins, Henry, Sam Ford, and Joshua Green (2013) *Spreadable Media: Creating Value and Meaning in a Networked Culture*. New York: New York University Press.

Jenkins, Henry, Ravi Purushotma, Katie Clinton, Margaret Weigel, and Alice J. Robison (2006) *Confronting the Challenges of Participatory*

*Culture Media Education for the Twenty-First Century*. Chicago: MacArthur Foundation.

Johnson, Michael, Jr. (2014) 'The It Gets Better Project: A Study in (and of) Whiteness – in LGBT Youth and Media Cultures'. *Queer Youth and Media Cultures*. Ed. Christopher Pullen. London: Palgrave Macmillan, pp. 278–91.

June, Laura (2017) 'YouTube has a Fake Peppa Pig Problem'. *The Outline*. 16 March. Available at: https://theoutline.com/post/1239/youtube-has-a-fake-peppa-pig-problem

Kafka, Peter (2014) 'It's Over! Viacom and Google Settle YouTube Lawsuit'. *Recode*, 18 March. Available at: https://www.recode.net/2014/3/18/11624656/its-over-viacom-and-google-settle-youtube-lawsuit

Karnitschnig, Matthew (2007) 'New Viacom deal takes swipe at YouTube', *The Wall Street Journal*, 20 February, p. B12. Accessed via Factiva database.

Karnitschnig, Matthew and Kevin Delaney (2006) 'Media Titans Pressure YouTube Over Copyrights'. *The Wall Street Journal*, 14 October, p. A3. Accessed via Factiva database.

Kastrenakes, Jacob (2016) 'YouTube's New Plan to Deal with Awful Comments: Have Commenters Help Moderate'. *The Verge*, 21 September. Available at: https://www.theverge.com/2016/9/21/13001520/youtube-heroes-comment-moderation-program-announced

Keen, Andrew (2007) *The Cult of the Amateur: How Today's Internet is Killing Our Culture*. New York: Random House.

Kerwin, Ann Marie (2006) 'NBC Doesn't Believe in Viral'. *Advertising Age* 77(9): 51.

Kirsner, Scott (2005) 'Now Playing: Your Home Video'. *The New York Times*, New York, 27 October. Accessed via Factiva database.

Kleeman, David (2015) 'YouTube Kids: Implication for the Kids Media Industries'. *Huffington Post*: The Blog. Published 26 February 2015. Available at: http://www.huffingtonpost.com/david-kleeman/youtube-kids-implications_1_b_6763714.html

Knight, Brooke A. (2000) 'Watch Me! Webcams and the Public Exposure of Private Lives'. *Art Journal* 59(4): 21–5.

Knobel, Michele and Colin Lankshear (2014) 'Studying New Literacies'. *Journal of Adolescent and Adult Literacy* 58(2): 97–101.

Kolaki, Rosie (2017) 'These Drama Channels are Causing a Huge Storm on YouTube for the Wrong Reasons'. *We the Unicorns*, 28 March. Available at: http://www.wetheunicorns.com/youtubers/drama-channels-youtube/

Kopytoff, Verne (2006). 'Copyright questions dog YouTube / Deals with entertainment industry limit site's liability'. *The San Francisco Chronicle*, San Francisco, 27 October, p. D1.

Kornblum, Janet (2006) 'Now Playing on YouTube'. *USA Today*, 18 July. Available at: http://www.usatoday.com/tech/news/2006-07-17-digital-download-youtube_x.htm

Koskela, Hille (2004) 'Webcams, TV Shows and Mobile Phones: Empowering Exhibitionism'. *Surveillance and Society* 2(2/3): 199–215.

Kranz, Cindy (2008) 'Schools take stance on bullying: Pushed by state law, and public incidents, districts crack down'. *The Enquirer*, Cincinnati [online] 2 March. Accessed 31 March 2008 from http://news.enquirer.com/apps/pbcs.dll/article?AID=/20080302/NEWS0102/803020345

Kumar, Sangeet (2016). 'YouTube Nation: Precarity and Agency in India's Online Video Scene'. *International Journal of Communication* 10: 5608–5625.

Lange, Patricia G. (2007a) 'Commenting on Comments: Investigating Responses to Antagonism on YouTube'. Paper presented at *Society for Applied Anthropology Conference*, Tampa, Florida.

— (2007b) 'Publicly private and privately public: Social networking on YouTube'. *Journal of Computer-Mediated Communication* 13(1): 361–80.

— (2007c) 'The Vulnerable Video Blogger: Promoting Social Change Through Intimacy'. *The Scholar and Feminist Online* 5(2). Available at: http://www.barnard.edu/sfonline/blogs/lange_01.htm

— (2014) *Kids on YouTube: Technical identities and digital literacies.* Walnut Creek, CA: Left Coast Press.

Letzing, John (2007) 'UPDATE: Google Unveils Copyright Protection Tools For YouTube'. *Dow Jones Business News*, 16 October. Accessed via Factiva database.

Li, Kenneth (2006) 'Viacom asks YouTube to purge certain clips'. *Reuters News*, 31 October. Accessed via Factiva database.

Livingstone, Sonia (2004) 'Media Literacy and the Challenge of New Information and Communication Technologies'. *The Communication Review* 7, pp. 3–14.

Livingstone, Sonia, Elizabeth Van Couvering, and Nancy Thumim (2008) 'Converging traditions of research on media and information literacies'. *Handbook of Research on New Literacies*. Eds Julie Coiro et al. New York: Lawrence Earlbaum and Associations, pp. 103–32.

Lobato, Ramon (2016) 'The cultural logic of digital intermediaries: YouTube multichannel networks'. *Convergence* 22(4): 348–60.

— (2017) 'Rethinking International TV Flows: Research in the Age of Netflix'. *Television and New Media*, online first DOI: 10.1177/1527476417708245, pp. 1–16.

Lotz, Amanda D. (2007) *The Television Will be Revolutionized*. New York and London: New York University Press.

McCosker, Anthony (2014) 'Trolling as provocation: YouTube's agonistic publics'. *Convergence: Journal of New Media Technologies* 20(2): 201–17.

McIntyre, Hugh (2017) 'Report: YouTube is the Most Popular Site of On-Demand Music Streaming'. *Forbes*, 27 September. Available at: https://www.forbes.com/sites/hughmcintyre/2017/09/27/the-numbers-prove-it-the-world-is-listening-to-the-music-it-loves-on-youtube/

Mckee, Alan (2011) 'YouTube versus the National Film and Sound Archive: Which is the more useful resource for historians of Australian television?' *Television and New Media* 12(2): 154–73.

McKenna, Barrie (2006) 'At YouTube, a Copyright Conundrum Continues'. *The Globe and Mail*, Canada, October 11, p. B1.

McRobbie, Angela and Jenny Garber (1976) 'Girls and Subcultures'. *Resistance Through Rituals: Youth Subcultures in Post-War Britain*. Eds Stuart Hall and Tony Jefferson. London: HarperCollins, pp. 209–29.

McRobbie, Angela and Sarah Thornton (2002) 'Rethinking "Moral Panic" for Multi-Mediated Social Worlds'. *Youth Justice: Critical Readings*. Eds John Muncie and Eugene Mclaughlin. London: Sage, pp. 68–79.

Marres, Noortje and Carolin Gerlitz (2016) 'Interface Methods: Renegotiating Relations between Digital Social Research, STS and Sociology'. *The Sociological Review* 64(1): 21–46.

Martinson, Jane (2006) 'Google faces copyright fight over YouTube'. *Guardian*, London, 13 October, p. 30.

— (2017) 'Guardian Pulls Ads from Google After They Were Placed Next to Extremist Material'. *Guardian*, 17 March. Available at: https://www.theguardian.com/media/2017/mar/16/guardian-pulls-ads-google-placed-extremist-material

Marvin, Ginny (2017) 'With Brand Safety in Mind, YouTube Steps Up Efforts to "Fight Online Terror"'. *Marketing Land*, 21 June. Available at: https://marketingland.com/brand-safety-youtube-efforts-fight-online-terror-218028

Marwick, Alice and Rebecca Lewis (2017) 'Media Manipulation and

Disinformation Online'. New York: Data and Society Research Institute. Available at: https://datasociety.net/output/media-manip ulation-and-disinfo-online/

Massanari, Adrienne (2017) '#Gamergate and The Fappening: How Reddit's algorithm, governance, and culture support toxic techno-cultures'. *New Media and Society* 19(3): 329–46.

Matthews, Nicole (2007) 'Confessions to a New Public: Video Nation Shorts'. *Media, Culture and Society* 29(3): 435–48.

Meikle, Graham (2002) *Future Active: Media Activism and the Internet.* Sydney: Pluto Press.

Mensel, Robert E. (1991) 'Kodakers Lying in Wait: Amateur Photography and the Right of Privacy in New York, 1885–1915'. *Arts Quarterly* 1(43): 24–45.

Miller, Claire Cain (2011) 'YouTube Acquires a Producer of Videos'. *The New York Times,* 7 March. Available at: http://www.nytimes.com/2011/03/08/technology/08youtube.html

Mills, Eleanor (2007) 'Viacom Sued Over Colbert Parody on YouTube'. *ZDNet,* 22 March. Available at: http://news.zdnet.com/2100-9595-6169765.html

Miltner, Kate and Tim Highfield (2017) 'Never Gonna GIF You Up: Analyzing the Cultural Significance of the Animated GIF'. *Social Media+ Society* 3(3): http://journals.sagepub.com/doi/abs/10.1177/2056305117725223

Mittell, Jason (2006) 'Narrative Complexity in Contemporary American Television'. *The Velvet Light Trap* 58: 29–40.

Morreale, Joanne (2014) 'From Homemade to Store Bought: Annoying Orange and the Professionalization of YouTube'. *Journal of Consumer Culture* 14(1): 113–128.

Morrissey, Brian (2006) 'Old Media Faces a Hard Lesson On Sharing'. *Adweek,* 3 April.

Moylan, Brian (2015) 'A Decade of YouTube Has Changed the Future of Television'. *Time,* 23 April. Available at: http://time.com/3828217/youtube-decade/

Murdock, Graham and Robin McCron (1976) 'Youth and Class: The Career of a Confusion'. *Working Class Youth Culture.* Eds Geoff Mungham and Geoff Pearson. London: Routledge and Kegan Paul, pp. 10–26.

Murphy, Candace (2006) 'Today's Kids Have their own Outlets for Creativity'. *The Oakland Tribune,* 22 July. Accessed via Factiva database.

Murray, Simone (2004) '"Celebrating the Story the Way it Is": Cultural Studies, Corporate Media and the Contested Utility of

Fandom'. *Continuum: Journal of Media and Cultural Studies* 1(18): 7–25.

Napoli, Philip and Robyn Caplan (2017) 'Why Media Companies Insist they're not Media Companies, Why they're Wrong, and why it Matters'. *First Monday* 22(5): https://journals.uic.edu/ojs/index.php/fm/article/view/7051.

Nazerali, Sanjay (2017) 'How YouTube Influencers are Rewriting the Marketing Rulebook'. *Huffington Post*, 2 Oct. Available at: http://www.huffingtonpost.com/entry/how-youtube-influencers-are-rewriting-the-marketing_us_59d2b250e4b03905538d17c3

Nead, Lynda (2004) 'Animating the Everyday: London on Camera Circa 1900'. *Journal of British Studies* 1(43): 65–90.

Niemeyer, Dodie J. and Hannah R. Gerber (2015) 'Maker Culture and Minecraft: Implications for the Future of Learning'. *Educational Media International* 52(3): 216–26.

Nightingale, Virginia (2007) 'The Cameraphone and Online Image Sharing'. *Continuum: Journal of Media and Cultural Studies* 21(2): 289–301.

Noguchi, Yuke and Sara Kehaulani Goo (2006) 'To the Media, YouTube Is a Threat and a Tool'. *The Washington Post*, 31 October. Accessed via Factiva database.

Nussenbaum, Evelyn, Oliver Ryan, and Peter Lewis (2005) Media on the cutting edge. *Fortune* 152(11): 217.

O'Brien, Sarah Ashley (2017) 'YouTube and Syria: Tech's Role as Archivist'. *CNN Tech*, 24 August. Available at: http://money.cnn.com/2017/08/24/technology/culture/youtube-syria-videos/index.html

O'Reilly, Tim (2005) 'What is Web 2.0? Design Patterns and Business Models for the Next Generation of Software'. *O'Reilly Network*. Available at: http://www.oreillynet.com/pub/a/oreilly/tim/news/2005/09/30/what-is-web-20.html

Paolillo, John C. (2008) 'Structure and Network in the YouTube Core'. Paper presented at *41st Hawaii International Conference on System Sciences*.

Patchin, Justin W. and Sameer Hinduja (2006) 'Bullies Move Beyond the Schoolyard: A Preliminary Look At Cyberbullying'. *Youth Violence and Juvenile Justice* 4(2): 148–69.

Perez, Sarah (2017) 'YouTube's App is Dominating Mobile by Monthly Users, Time Spent'. *TechCrunch*, 13 September. Available at: https://techcrunch.com/2017/09/13/youtubes-app-is-dominating-mobile-video-by-monthly-users-time-spent/

Phillips, Whitney (2015) *This is Why We Can't Have Nice Things:*

*Mapping the Relationship Between Online Trolling and Mainstream Culture*. Cambridge, MA: MIT Press.

Plantin, Jean-Christophe, Carl Lagoze, Paul N. Edwards, and Christian Sandvig (2016) 'Infrastructure Studies Meet Platform Studies in the Age of Google and Facebook'. *New Media and Society* Online first doi: https://doi.org/10.1177/1461444816661553

Popper, Ben (2015) 'Red Dawn: An Inside Look at YouTube's New Ad-Free Subscription Service'. *The Verge*, 21 October. Available at: https://www.theverge.com/2015/10/21/9566973/youtube-red-ad-free-offline-paid-subscription-service

— (2017) 'YouTube TV Review: A DVR to Rule Them All'. *The Verge*, 5 April. Available at: https://www.theverge.com/2017/4/5/15177462/youtube-tv-review-streaming-cable-subscription-service

Postigo, Hector (2016) 'The socio-technical architecture of digital labor: Converting play into YouTube money'. *New Media and Society* 18(2): 332–49.

Potts, Jason, Stuart Cunningham, John Hartley, and Paul Ormerod (2008a) 'Social Network Markets: A New Definition of the Creative Industries'. *Journal of Cultural Economics* 32(3): 167–85.

Potts, Jason, John Hartley, John Banks, Jean Burgess, Rachel Cobcroft, Stuart Cunningham, and Lucy Montgomery (2008b) 'Consumer Co-Creation and Situated Creativity'. *Industry and Innovation* 15(5): 459–74.

Prelinger, Rick (2007) 'Archives and Access in the twenty-first century'. *Cinema Journal* 46(3): 114–18.

Prensky, Marc (2001a) 'Digital Natives, Digital Immigrants'. *On the Horizon* 9(5).

— (2001b) 'Digital Natives, Digital Immigrants'. *On the Horizon* 9(6).

Priddy, Molly (2017) 'Why is YouTube Demonetizing LGBTQ Videos?' *Autostraddle*, 22 September. Available at: https://www.autostraddle.com/why-is-youtube-demonetizing-lgbtqia-videos-395058/

Punathambekar, Aswin (2015) 'Satire, Elections, and Democratic Politics in Digital India'. *Television and New Media* 16(4): 394–400.

Ramadge, Andrew (2008) 'Why Party Boy Corey is a Genius'. *News.com.au*. Available at: http://www.news.com.au/story/0,23599,23066396-5015729,00.html

Rao, Leena (2016) 'YouTube CEO Says There's "No Timetable" for Profitability'. *Fortune*, 29 October. Available at: http://fortune.com/2016/10/18/youtube-profits-ceo-susan-wojcicki/

Raun, Tobias (2016) *Out Online: Trans Self-Representation and Community Building on YouTube*. Oxford and New York: Routledge.

Rawstorne, Tom and Brad Crouch (2006) 'The Free-for-All Called

YouTube'. *The Sunday Mail*, Australia, 15 October. Accessed via Factiva database.

Rieder, Bernhard, Ariadna Matamoros-Fernández, and Oscar Coromina (2017) 'From Ranking Algorithms to "Ranking Cultures": Investigating the Modulation of Visibility in YouTube Search Results'. *Convergence*, forthcoming (final author version cited).

Rimmer, Matthew (2017) 'The Dancing Baby: Copyright Law, YouTube, and Music Videos'. *Research Handbook on Intellectual Property in Media and Entertainment*. Eds Megan Richardson and Sam Ricketson. Cheltenham, UK, Northampton, MA: Edward Elgar, pp. 150–94.

Rose, Richard (2005) 'Language, Soft Power and Asymmetrical Internet Communication'. *Oxford Internet Institute Research Report No. 7*. Available at: http://www.oii.ox.ac.uk/research/project.cfm?id=7

Ross, Andrew (2000) 'The Mental Labor Problem'. *Social Text* 2(18): 1–31.

Rossiter, Ned (2016) *Software, Infrastructure, Labor: A Media Theory of Logistical Nightmares*. London, New York: Routledge.

Rowan, David (2005) 'The Next Big Thing: Video-Sharing Websites; Trendsurfing'. *The Times*, London, 19 November, Magazine, p. 14.

Ryan, Oliver (2006) 'Don't Touch That Dial'. *Fortune* 154(5): 76–7.

Sánchez-Olmos, Cande and Eduardo Vinuela (2017) 'The Musicless Music Video as a Spreadale Meme Video: Format, User inteaction, and Meaning on YouTube'. *International Journal of Communication* (11)21. Available at: http://ijoc.org/index.php/ioc/article/view/6410

Schilt, Kristen (2003) '"A Little Too Ironic": The Appropriation and Packaging of Riot Grrrl Politics By Mainstream Female Musicians'. *Popular Music and Society* 26(10): 5–16.

Schroeder, Stan (2012). 'YouTube Opens Partner Program to Everyone'. *Mashable*, 13 April. Available at: http://mashable.com/2012/04/13/youtube-opens-partner-program

Seavers, Kris (2017) 'YouTubers warn: The 'adpocalypse' is here – and it's killing them'. *The Daily Dot*, 18 September. Available at: https://www.dailydot.com/upstream/youtube-adpocalypse/

Segev, Elad, Niv Ahituv, and Karine Barzilai-Nahon (2007) 'Mapping Diversities and Tracing Trends of Cultural Homogeneity/Heterogeneity in Cyberspace'. *Journal of Computer-Mediated Communication* 12(12): 69–97.

Seiberling, Grace and Carolyn Bloore (1986) *Amateurs, Photography, and the Mid-Victorian Imagination*. Chicago: University of Chicago Press.

Senft, Theresa M. (2008) *Camgirls: Celebrity and Community in the Age of Social Networks*. New York: Peter Lang.

— (2013) 'Microcelebrity and the Branded Self'. *A Companion to New Media Dynamics*. Eds John Hartley, Jean Burgess, and Axel Bruns. London: Wiley-Blackwell, pp. 346–54.

Serazio, Michael and Brooke Erin Duffy (2017) 'Social Media Marketing'. *The Sage Handbook of Social Media*. Eds Jean Burgess, Alice Marwick, and Thomas Poell. London: Sage, pp. 481–96.

Shah, Chirag and Gary Marchionini (2007) 'Preserving 2008 US Presidential Election Videos'. Paper presented at *IWAW'07*, Vancouver, British Columbia, Canada.

Shefrin, Elana (2004) '*Lord of the Rings, Star Wars*, and Participatory Fandom: Mapping New Congruences Between the Internet and Media Entertainment Culture'. *Critical Studies in Media Communication* 21(3): 261–81.

Shifman, Limor (2014) *Memes in Digital Culture*. Cambridge, MA: MIT Press.

Shirky, Clay (2008) *Here Comes Everybody: The Power of Organizing Without Organizations*. New York: Penguin.

Shribman, Bill (2015). 'YouTube Kids New App: The Experts Weigh In'. *GeekDad*. Published 1 March 2015. Available at: http://geekdad.com/2015/03/youtubes-new-kids-app/

Slonje, Rober and Peter K. Smith (2008) 'Cyberbullying: Another main type of bullying?' *Scandinavian Journal of Psychology* 49(2): 147–54.

Smit, Rik, Ansgard Heinrich, and Marcel Broersma (2017) 'Witnessing in the new memory ecology: Memory construction of the Syrian conflict on YouTube'. *New Media and Society* 19(2): 289–307.

Smith, Bridie (2007) 'Schools Ban YouTube Sites in Cyber-Bully Fight'. *The Age*, Melbourne. 2 March. Available at: http://www.theage.com.au/

Smith, Daniel (2014) 'Charlie is so "English"-like: Nationality and the Branded Celebrity Person in the Age of YouTube'. *Celebrity Studies* 5(3): 256–274.

Snickars, Pelle and Patrick Vonderau (2009) Eds. *The YouTube Reader*. Stockholm: National Library of Sweden.

Soha, Michael and Zachary McDowell (2017) 'Monetizing a Meme: YouTube, Content ID, and the Harlem Shake'. *Social Media+ Society* 2(1): http://journals.sagepub.com/doi/abs/10.1177/2056305115623801

Solomon, Leron (2015) 'Fair Users or Content Abusers? The Automatic

Flagging of Non-Infringing Videos by Content ID on YouTube'. *Hofstra Law Review* 44(1): 237–68.

Springhall, John (1999) *Youth, Popular Culture and Moral Panics: Penny Gaffs to Gangsta Rap, 1830–1997*. London: Palgrave Macmillan.

Spurgeon, Christina (2008) *Advertising and New Media*. London and New York: Routledge.

Stein, Joel (2006) 'Straight Outta Narnia'. *Time* 167(17): 69.

Stevenson, Nick (2003a) *Cultural Citizenship: Cosmopolitan Questions*. Maidenhead: Open University Press.

— (2003b) 'Cultural Citizenship in the "Cultural" Society: A Cosmopolitan Approach'. *Citizenship Studies* 3(7): 331–48.

Stone, Brad (2007), 'Young Turn to Web Sites Without Rules'. *New York Times*, 2 January. Available at: http://www.nytimes.com/2007/01/02/technology/02net.htm.

Storey, John (2003) *Inventing Popular Culture: From Folklore to Globalization*. Malden, MA and Oxford: Blackwell.

Strangelove, Michael (2010) *Watching YouTube: Extraordinary videos by ordinary people*. Toronto: University of Toronto Press.

Street, Brian (1984) *Literacy in Theory and Practice*. Cambridge: Cambridge University Press.

Suciu, Peter (2007) 'YouTube Goes Local With 9 Country-Specific Versions', *TechCrunch*, 19 June. Available at: https://techcrunch.com/2007/06/19/youtube-goes-local-with-9-country-specific-versions/

Swartz, Jon (2007) 'YouTube Gets Media Providers' Help Foiling Piracy'. *USA Today*, 16 October, p. B4.

Terranova, Tiziana (2000) 'Free Labor: Producing Culture for the Digital Economy'. *Social Text* 2(18): 33–58.

Thompson, John B. (2005) 'The New Visibility'. *Theory, Culture and Society* 22(6): 31–51.

Tracey, Michael (1998) *The Decline and Fall of Public Service Broadcasting*. Oxford and New York: Oxford University Press.

Turner, Fred (2006) *From Counterculture to Cyberculture: Steward Brand, the Whole Earth Network and the Rise of Digital Utopianism*. Chicago: Chicago University Press.

Turner, Graeme (2004) *Understanding Celebrity*. London: Sage.

— (2006) 'The Mass Production of Celebrity: "Celetoids", Reality TV and the "Demotic Turn"'. *International Journal of Cultural Studies* 2(9): 153–66.

van Dijck, José (2013). *The Culture of Connectivity: A Critical History of Social Media*. Oxford: Oxford University Press.

van Dijck, José and Thomas Poell (2013) 'Understanding Social Media Logic'. *Media and Communication* 1(1): 2–14.

Vascellaro, Jessica E., Amir Efrati, and Ethan Smith (2011) 'YouTube Recasts for New Viewers'. *Wall Street Journal*, 7 April. Available at: http://www.wsj.com/articles/SB1000142405274870401360457624706094091310 4

Veiga, Alex (2006) 'Anti-Piracy System Could Hurt YouTube'. *Associated Press Newswires*, 13 October. Accessed via Factiva database.

Von Hippel, Eric (2005) *Democratizing Innovation*. Cambridge, MA: The MIT Press.

Wallenstein, Andrew (2006a) 'Biz not sure how to treat upstart YouTube'. *The Hollywood Reporter*, 21 March. Available at: http://www.hollywoodreporter.com/hr/search/article_display.jsp?vnu_content_id=1002199881

— (2006b) 'MTV2 embraces embattered YouTube video-sharing site'. *Reuters News*, 3 March. Accessed via Factiva database.

Waxman, Sharon (2011) 'YouTube Unveils Original Content Channels in Challenge to TV'. *The Wrap*, 28 October. Available at: http://www.thewrap.com/youtube-launch-dozens-original-content-channels-challenging-television-32297/

Weinberger, David (2007) *Everything is Miscellaneous: The Power of the New Digital Disorder*. New York: Times Books.

Whelan, Ella (2017) '#metoo: A Moral Panic About Men'. 18 October. Available at: http://www.spiked-online.com/newsite/article/metoo-a-moral-panic-about-men

Wikström, Patrik (2013) 'The Dynamics of Digital Multisided Media Markets'. *A Companion to New Media Dynamics*. Eds John Hartley, Jean Burgess, and Axel Bruns. London: Wiley-Blackwell, pp. 231–46.

Williams, Raymond (1958) 'Culture is Ordinary'. *Resources of Hope. Culture, Democracy, Socialism*. Ed. Robin Gable (1989). London: Verso, pp. 3–18.

YouTube (2017a) Community Guidelines, 8 October. Available at: https://www.youtube.com/yt/policyandsafety/communityguidelines.html

YouTube (2017b) What is fair use?, 8 October. Available at: https://www.youtube.com/yt/copyright/fair-use.html

YouTube Official Blog (2010) 'Broadcast Yourself'. 18 March. Available at: https://youtube.googleblog.com/2010/03/broadcast-yourself.html

YouTube Creator Blog (2017) 'Introducing Expanded YouTube Partner Program Safeguards to Protect Creators'. 6 April. Available at: https://youtube-creators.googleblog.com/2017/04/introducing-expanded-youtube-partner.html

YouTube Engineering and Developers Blog (2015) 'YouTube Now

Defaults to HTML5 <video>'. 27 January. Available at: https://you
tube-eng.googleblog.com/2015/01/youtube-now-defaults-to-html5_
27.html

Zimmermann, Patricia (1995) *Reel Families: A Social History of
Amateur Film*. Bloomington: Indiana University Press.

Zittrain, Jonathan (2008) *The Future of the Internet and How to Stop It*.
New Haven: Yale University Press.

# Index